The Vivekananda HANDBOOK FOR Everyday Living

REVISED EDITION

ANSHUL CHATURVEDI

BLOOMSBURY
NEW DELHI • LONDON • OXFORD • NEW YORK • SYDNEY

BLOOMSBURY INDIA
Bloomsbury Publishing India Pvt. Ltd
Second Floor, LSC Building No. 4, DDA Complex, Pocket C – 6 & 7,
Vasant Kunj, New Delhi, 110070

BLOOMSBURY, BLOOMSBURY INDIA and the Diana logo
are trademarks of Bloomsbury Publishing Plc

First published in India 2021
This revised edition published 2025

ISBN: PB: 978-93-69523-70-2; ebook: 978-93-89611-38-0
2 4 6 8 10 9 7 5 3 1

Typeset in Manipal Technologies Limited
Printed and bound in India by Gopsons Papers Pvt. Ltd., Noida

FSC www.fsc.org
MIX
Paper | Supporting responsible forestry
FSC® C191020

Praise for *The Vivekananda Handbook for Everyday Living*

'Reading Vivekananda is an infusion of strength and positivity. In his uniquely honest, relatable and personal style, the author channels Vivekananda in a way that is grounded yet inspiring. I highly recommend *The Vivekananda Handbook for Everyday Living* to one and all.'

Swami Sarvapriyananda,
Head of the Vedanta Society of New York

'Anshul's book is a gentle yet powerful companion for anyone who seeks to undertake the journey from the always-busy outer world to the calm of the inner self. We are all caught up in life's constant demands – work, family, responsibilities – and end up mostly entangled, restless and unfulfilled. There is often an emptiness within despite abundance, but there is a desperate restlessness when you don't have what you want.

And then, you read a few pages of this book, and it immediately invites you to pause, to take a deep breath, to turn inwards, where a deeper calm awaits. Suddenly, all that seemed so urgent and pressing seems trivial. This book, while grounded in the realities of everyday life, lights the way along Swami Vivekananda's path and takes you closer to a process of inner awakening. I have read and experienced it – now, it is your turn!'

Manoj Bajpayee, Actor

The Vivekananda HANDBOOK FOR Everyday Living

Contents

Introduction

'I DO NOT CARE *for human help.*'

In the 17 years of life that I had lived till that point of time, this was the most absolute sentence I had ever read. With that one thought, Swami Vivekananda gatecrashed my teen mind, and hasn't vacated it since.

'I do not care for human help' got embedded into my consciousness and slowly crystallised into an idea when I was at an impressionable age, trying to figure out what my disjointed, dreamy, dysfunctional life was all about. And despite the years dimming the sharpness of my mind, the edginess of this idea has not faded a bit.

It is not easy to explain how deeply an idea like this influences the way one thinks. For the last 30 years, this thought, this basic concept of 'not caring for human help' has unsettled – not in a way I regret – my mind.

Let me offer a visual parallel to explain what holding on to an idea like that for so long feels like. Think of the last time when you saw, in an action movie, a high-octane car chase where someone is holding on precariously to a recklessly driven high-speed car, grasping the bonnet or the roof as the music pulsates and the car sways from one direction to another. Holding on is tough, but once you are in that situation, letting go seems an even more unsettling option.

Holding on to that thought has been a bit like that.

Holding on to it means being comfortable with being a social misfit from 17 all the way to 47, and still counting. It means having a comfort level with being that misfit, that recluse – and with this sentiment only increasing with time.

It means not being concerned, teenage years onwards, about whether you are part of the cool gang or the uncool gang or no gang at all. It means having no expectation of your buddies or anyone else rushing to your aid when you're in trouble. It means not having any shoulders to cry on. It means learning to handle your troubles *on your own*.

It means shunning events and get-togethers you don't really want to be at, whether hosted by acquaintances or relatives, and being comfortable with the occasional sniping which follows on that account.

It means rejecting references for securing a job. It means being okay with walking out of your cushy job in a huff and thereby turning jobless and cashless at 27, and then saying a polite 'no' to a 'friend' who promises that his influential dad will talk to people and get your job back.

It doesn't mean always knowing what you are going to do, but it does mean almost always knowing what you are *not* going to do. It means asking yourself, when faced with difficult choices, the point Vivekananda made, 'If we do not have the Ganges, will we drink gutter water?'

It means a basic comfort level with anonymity. Or, occasionally, a degree of comfort, even familiarity, with the reverse – the unwanted spotlight. It means so much less stress – no networking, no lobbying, no pressure to be popular in the real or the virtual world, no effort to click the perfect selfie, no great inclination to gather or retain followers, either real or virtual, no regret at lack of connectivity or social skills, no investments in climbing the social ladder, no keeping people happy since they may at some point in life be of use to you.

Why would you look to cultivate people who may help you when you *do not care for human help*?

You're, therefore, sort of free.

It's a freedom that comes at a price, yes.

But once you *do* get used to it, it's addictive – you won't let it go. When I look back at things, the day I got well and truly addicted to it was, in a very individual sense, my Independence Day.

Come, let me take you through my emotional freedom struggle.

You Don't Have to 'Follow' Vivekananda to 'Get' This

> *Thus has wisdom more secret than all secrets, been declared to thee by Me. Having reflected on it fully, do as thou choosest.* (Bhagvad Gita, XVIII.63)

Why should you even pick up something like this?

You are not looking to join the Ramakrishna Mission or embrace the life of a monk. Neither am I. So why should I write – and why must you read – anything about Vivekananda? Or, for that matter, about anyone like him – a preacher, monk and philosopher who never had to live an ordinary life full of drudgery, struggle and heartbreak. 'Other wordly' is the phrase commonly used to describe such lifestyles now. Not of our world. How, then, is such a life relevant to us?

Yes, presidents and prime ministers quote him – but then, unlike them, we don't have to think about world peace, harmony and global understanding. Philosophers from Romain Rolland to Rabindranath Tagore gush about him – but we are neither interpreters of philosophy nor teachers of the mysteries of the universe.

What did he teach that would make sense, *real* sense, to us?

Actually, what Vivekananda thought or taught in 1895 or 1905 isn't the point at all.

The point is what *we* make of his teachings.

Many of us with a strong sense of individuality dislike 'following' any leader or philosopher, since it means laying aside our own intellect and understanding of the world and embracing a life prescribed by a supposedly 'superior' mind.

All evolved minds have first raised questions and expressed doubts before putting their faith in a thought. A certain degree of intellectual arrogance is required to understand and assimilate the best points of higher thought – because such understanding comes only after thorough questioning.

A timid, servile mind may simply accept, unfiltered, whatever the supposed higher thought is. But that is senseless and demeaning to oneself. Krishna himself, after explaining life's fundamentals at length to Arjuna, told him to think it over and *do as he deemed fit.* When it comes to understanding a philosophy of life, no matter how brilliantly articulated, it is essential to probe and ponder before accepting it.

We don't have to worship him, or follow him blindly, to learn from his life

- Many of us with a strong sense of individuality dislike 'following' any leader or philosopher. That would mean putting aside our intellect and understanding of the world and embracing a life prescribed by a 'superior' mind.
- Krishna himself, after explaining to Arjuna the fundamentals of life, told him to think it over and do as he deemed fit. A philosophy of life, no matter how brilliantly explained, must be probed and pondered before being accepted.

- The core of Vivekananda's teachings is the independence of thought. There are many elements of what he wrote that I relate to. And many that I can't relate to.
- Through his teachings, I seek clarity to follow the path that I opt to live by. Through this book, I want to simplify his core philosophy and show how he impacted my life.

The core of Vivekananda's teachings is the *independence* of thought. There are many elements of what he wrote that I totally relate to. Yet there are equally, many specifics in his writings and discussions that I can never relate to or implement; perhaps they made sense in the context of time and place when he made those points, but I do not see myself blindly accepting them all, no matter how highly I rate the intellectual and emotional robustness of Vivekananda. I do not wish to *replicate* his thinking or how he lived his life. I seek instead to find, through his teachings, the clarity to better follow the path that *I* opt to live by.

Subhas Chandra Bose wrote, 'If Swami*ji* had been alive today, he would have been my guru, that is to say, I would have accepted him as my Master.' This is a sentiment I identify with. But it does not mean that I will worship every word he uttered. More than *what* he thought, *how* he thought engages and intrigues me.

Sister Nivedita spoke of him, after he was no more, in these words:

> *The truths he preaches would have been as true, had he never been born. Nay more, they would have been equally authentic. The difference would have lain in their difficulty of access, in their want of modern clearness and incisiveness of statement, and in their loss of mutual coherence and unity. Had he not lived, texts that today will carry the*

bread of life to thousands might have remained the obscure disputes of scholars. He taught with authority, and not as one of the Pundits. For he himself had plunged to the depths of the realisation which he preached, and he came back like Ramanuja only to tell its secrets to the pariah, the outcast, and the foreigner.

What Vivekananda does is bring things out of the realm of the 'obscure disputes of scholars'. He teaches with simplicity, and with authority. And he plunges into the depths of things and comes back to tell us their secrets as well, irrespective of whether we are outcasts or foreigners or just cynical observers. Through this book, in my own limited way, I am trying to do for Vivekananda's writings what the monk had done for scholarly texts – simplify the core philosophy and explain how it impacted my life.

You Don't Have to be 'Religious' for Vivekananda to Help You

For those relatively – or completely – unfamiliar with what the Swami's mind was about, when they see the odd book on him lying around on my table, or are told that 'he is quite a consumer of Vivekananda's writings', a natural reaction is for them to say, 'Ahh, so you're a *religious* sort of person.'

Umm, no.

You *don't* have to be religious to understand or follow Vivekananda. You could be an atheist or agnostic and still find a great connect with his thoughts. Or you could be a head priest at a temple on the ghats of Varanasi and yet take umbrage at many of the outrageous thoughts expressed in the Swami's fluent, often acidic English.

The one thing that really attracted me to Vivekananda, and the reason why I kept taking the risk of being seen with Vivekananda's works in my hands even at an age when being called 'religious' was sort of a 'poor chap' comment, really, was the utter absence of middle-class morality in his thinking.

The way society, middle-class India in particular, interprets 'moral' and 'good' and 'religious' sentiments can sometimes be quite disconcerting. By reflex, the 'good' people often promptly down their windows when they sense trouble in the neighbourhood. The instinct of 'keeping out of trouble' pulls at us. Bound by it, we are occasionally unable to distinguish between being good and being merely not evil.

Vivekananda would not have us be that sort of passive 'good'. For him, fear was a sin, and life, temporary. He wanted us to be willing to risk, to grow, to not be lost in seeking safety; for safety is an illusion. He reminded us that he planned little and took on great challenges. He would gently reprimand us in his acerbic, sharp prose if he found us lapsing into a tepid, politically correct existence. He would ask us to reconnect with the fiery, combative, let-the-world-do-what-it-will tone of his ideology. He would push us out of our comfort zones and make us think beyond earning our daily bread.

If we took shelter in declaring that we are nice, rule-abiding folk, he would probably dismiss that and push us to step out of our timidity: 'It is not law that we want, but the ability to break law. We want to be outlaws. If you are bound by laws, you will be a lump of clay. Whether you are beyond the law is not the question; but the thought that we are beyond law – upon that is based the whole history of humanity,' he would challenge.

I did not get drawn to Vivekananda because he fitted in with my middle-class basics and the outlines of what being 'good' meant there. I consumed him because he offered me a refreshing break from that safe zone, because he challenged most of the basics that I would otherwise have grown to absorb and unquestioningly accept.

If I hadn't picked up his thoughts at the age of 16 or so, I would have probably grown up to be a normal, nice, social, perfectly respectable middle-class professional and spent a lifetime thinking along all the lines that one is 'supposed to'.

Vivekananda for me, is *not* a religious icon to be worshipped. He is a brilliantly effective transmitter of a philosophy, a mindset.

I did not aim to shave my head and join a monastic order to replicate how he lived. Neither did I look to live out a regular 9-to-6 mechanical middle-class existence and simply add a photo of his to the deities gracing the pooja corner of my flat and wave an incense stick around him briefly each morning. I sought to live his approach *while* earning my daily bread, to tinge life's drudgery with a certain amount of flamboyance, not through lifestyle, but through my mind. The way a tycoon flaunts his cars and houses – that's the way I sort of flaunted my Vivekananda-tinged fundamentals: unapologetically, aggressively; to live what looked like a regular existence externally, but with a volatile philosophy simmering inside.

Vivekananda, the outspoken disruptor of 'middle-class morality'

The one thing that really attracted me to Vivekananda was the utter absence of middle-class morality in his thinking. He offered me a refreshing break, because he challenged most of the basics that I would otherwise grow to absorb and unquestioningly accept. If I hadn't picked up his thoughts at the age of 16, I would have probably grown up to be a normal, nice, social, perfectly respectable middle-class professional. Vivekananda for me is an effective transmitter of a philosophy, a mindset.

I sought to live his approach while earning my daily bread, to tinge life's drudgery with a certain amount of flamboyance, not through a lifestyle, but through my mind.

Long ago, when I was still exploring and assessing the degree of compatibility of the monk's mindset with mine, a single thought got embedded in my mind, like a splinter of wood from an unfinished piece of furniture sometimes gets embedded under a fingernail.

The thought was:

> *The older I grow, the more everything seems to me to lie in manliness. This is my new gospel. Do even evil like a man. Be wicked, if you must, on a grand scale!*

Which 'man of god' wearing saffron preaches *this*?

My first thought when I read this was how the most flamboyant cinematic villains were cult figures in their own right, whether it was Gabbar or Mogambo, the Joker or Darth Vader. Being wicked – when practised on a grand scale – did, oddly enough, seem a fairly popular, even aspirational, activity. I had often wondered about some of these pristine-pure genteel characters in the epics: Vibheeshan was good; Nakul and Sehdev were good; Bharat and Shatrughan were good. But yet Ravana had a greater recall than, say, Shatrughan, even though the latter could never be faulted for having crossed the line of correctness. Is it that grandeur and flamboyance – even if manifested in wickedness – hold a fascination for the human mind? Do we not applaud the flamboyant outlaw and anti-hero in movie after movie, often ahead of a 'nice' character with less strength of personality? Perhaps, at a basic level, Vivekananda had it right – do not aspire to be on the side of the wrong rather than the right, but, *if you must*, it is better to be wicked on a grand scale than to be nice in an ambivalent, lukewarm kind of way.

A clarification: One small point, so that what he said is not lost in transmission a century later. Vivekananda often resorts to the colloquial usage of his time to make a point, but it is not *literal*, not in gender terms at least. 'Manliness' does not refer to the alpha male. Neither is 'Like a man' about machismo, biceps or swearing. These phrases are politically incorrect when seen by today's benchmarks but this usage generally appears across his teachings, whether he was writing to a male associate or addressing a group of male disciples. When I read his fiery words, I am not seeking anything unique to 'men' – his 'manliness' means fighting off your fears, it means the absence of timidity, of hesitation, of an excessively strong instinct of self-preservation. Being a 'man' in this usage denotes a courageous *individual*, whether you identify with any gender, or with none, or with both. That is inconsequential here.

To resume: So, does following Vivekananda brand you as a God-fearing, 'religious' person?

Not really. Whether you pray twice each day or are an atheist, the takeaway from what he says is not very different.

'From Age 17 Onwards, He Has Helped Me Navigate Life'

Vivekananda's philosophy would have meant nothing to me if I could not have applied it practically. I am not so much a *student* of Vivekananda, but a *practitioner* of his ideas, applying some of them as and when my daily experiences offer the scope to do so, to the degree my understanding allows.

I did not study or analyse all that he did or said. I searched only for what helped me navigate my everyday life.

In my teens and twenties, the absorption was easiest. There wasn't so much analysis, but more of reflex and instinct, for at that age, you tend to be more impulsive. The odd thing in my case was that I wasn't a rebel tamed by a saffron-clad monk, but a docile, sickly, horribly unsocial child, an only child at that, who would avoid walking up to anyone anywhere if it could be helped, and who would rather jump off the school balcony than get on to the stage to give a speech. Vivekananda *made* me a teen rebel – following the sort of rebellion that does not rely on how much hair you have on your head or how sculpted your biceps are – but of the kind that tends to be age-proof and goes on, and on. Between 17 and 47, it is now some 30 years of cherry-picking ideas and thoughts from the 39 years of Vivekananda's lifespan. The rebellion ebbs and flows, but it's there, all the time.

A quick-to-fear teenager, I hated conflict, feared the dark, and was petrified of closed spaces in lifts. I would look over my shoulder when walking late at night. 'Fear is the greatest sin my religion teaches' – this is the most profound lesson that Vivekananda taught, repeatedly. I still hate lifts, but most of the fears of my childhood burnt themselves out through the teens and twenties. If I was afraid of getting on to a stage, I ensured I did it, over and over. If a densely forested area gave me the creeps, I forced myself to go there after sunset and stand still where it felt the creepiest.

Seeing fear as a sin, and at the apex of the list of sins, I tried to step up to conquer it in as many small battles as I could. Those battles dominated my growing years.

The defiant 'I don't care' tone of the cocky youngster was something I tried to assimilate, as a simple statement of fact. Let this or that happen, I *actually* don't care, I will handle what happens when it happens – that turned out to be a better handler of anxiety than all the books good old Dale Carnegie wrote on how to stop worrying and start living.

Indeed, I stopped 70 per cent of my worrying after I started reading Vivekananda.

Given the state of my mind as I entered my teens, I would probably have crashed from stress-related disorders in my twenties had I not followed Vivekananda. His words, 'I will die a thousand deaths rather than lead a jellyfish existence and yield to every requirement of this foolish world', helped me fight many moments when my more hesitant self, the side of me that hated conflict, would have probably preferred to 'adjust' and 'accommodate'. I would ask myself if I was getting into the reflex of 'leading a jellyfish existence' just to 'yield to every requirement' – this questioning was often deeply uncomfortable, for the answer was 'yes'. I taught myself to not worry so much about every requirement and learnt that there's no point fearing so much. Most things that kill us with fear aren't worth the stress, more so in hindsight.

Anyone can handle a comfortable existence. Vivekananda's prescription to handle an existence that is *not* so comfortable is quite simple – 'The Mother's child shall be a hero, a Mahavira. In unhappiness, sorrow, death and desolation, the Mother's child shall always remain fearless!'

'In unhappiness, sorrow, death and desolation' – If you work towards trying to be fearless here, in *these* situations, what else is left to plan for, to worry about? If we can use this as a reference point and manage half of what it would be to actually live like this, it would be the achievement of a lifetime.

But Vivekananda's thinking wasn't just bullheaded aggression.

A few days ago, I stumbled upon an old diary from 1991, when I was 18. Flipping through it was a disconcerting experience. By then, I had confronted some of life's questions and was acquainted with Vivekananda's writings. I had been writing pages upon pages of notes on death, addressing questions to myself, offering explanations on why I understood nothing any better after months of unsettled confusion – and then trashing those explanations. So sharp were the internal battles, so severe the doubts, that I am reasonably sure many considered me to be a little less than 'balanced' in those years. Some still do.

Those pages leave me wondering today how I retained some semblance of sanity through that phase. I think, in retrospect, that the clearest mind I had engaged with – Vivekananda's – had legitimized the angst of questioning without the need to seek immediate answers. An early page in my battered copy of *Letters of Swami Vivekananda* has this highlighted line, faded over time, '...[T]hat sort of regret and dissatisfaction is very good; it is the prelude to improvement. He who puts on a turban and immediately sees the Lord, progresses thus far and no farther. You are blessed indeed to have that constant dissatisfaction preying upon your mind – rest assured that there is no danger for you...'

Vivekananda made me see constant dissatisfaction as a growth trait, not as a psychological issue to be addressed. I, therefore, sought clarity even as I made peace with my doubts.

Fear must be fought.
Dissatisfaction must be welcomed.

As a practitioner of Vivekananda's ideas, I searched for what would help me navigate everyday life. A hesitant teenager at the outset who began seeing fear as a massive weakness, I ventured to conquer it in as many small battles as I could. Those battles dominated my growing years.

The Swami's words, 'I will die a thousand deaths rather than lead a jellyfish existence and yield to every requirement of this foolish world' helped me fight many moments when my more hesitant self would have probably chosen to adjust.

Vivekananda also made me see constant dissatisfaction as a growth trait, not as a psychological issue to be addressed.

The younger years also bring failure in large measure to some, if not to most of us. I had my share of failures. Most things that I had planned to do with my life at 19 were in a shambles by the time I was 24. And my mind was restless.

Despondent, often sleepless, with no one to turn to for help, I sat quietly and reflected on Vivekananda's words – 'Human help I spurn with my foot. He who has been with me through hills and dales, through deserts and forests, will be with me, I hope; if not, some heroic soul would arise some time or other, far abler than myself, and carry it out.'

I taught myself to get used to that basic idea – to stop beseeching for human help, to understand and accept that some things are not meant to be if He has decided they aren't.

I taught myself to get used to that basic idea – to stop beseeching for human help, to understand and accept that some things are *not* meant to be if He has decided they aren't. It is certainly not a lesson you learn in a day, but once you do, it is well worth the time spent on learning it.

The period between ages 24 and 40 (roughly), as it is for most, was the phase of entering and surviving the world outside. I had thought of many grand things I would do when I was just finishing school. I fancied my chances at making it big early in life, being a known name, either holding a position of power or a fancy pay cheque.

None of that happened.

My first jobs were teaching at a minuscule coaching centre and then working as a sub-editor at an unknown newspaper in an office tucked away in a lane in interior Jammu, while my friends and smarter cousins cracked the civil services, became doctors, or encashed their IIT+IIM pay cheques.

My ego and self-esteem did not take very well to all this.

I wondered whether that was how my life and career would turn out – mediocre. Then Vivekananda told me, in his usual forthright style – 'Do not be afraid of small beginnings, great things come afterwards. Be courageous.' I learnt, with difficulty, to not despair at small beginnings. And fought, with some success, the fear of being inconsequential and irrelevant.

Three quotes from Vivekananda that steadied me in tough times:

- Do not be afraid of small beginnings, great things come afterwards. Be courageous.
- Have faith that you are all, my brave lads, born to do great things! Let not the barks of puppies frighten you – no, not even the thunderbolts of heaven – but stand up and work!
- Tell my friends that a uniform silence is all my answer to my detractors. If I give them tit for tat, it would bring me down to a level with them. Tell them that truth will take care of itself.

When, through most of my twenties, neither what I did nor where I worked seemed to be flamboyant enough to fit in with my inflated opinion of myself, there were moments when the temptation to do things superficially began to kick in.

Drudgery, routine, a 'junior' status and the absence of both money and name are not great motivators. I caught myself grumbling. Vivekananda was quick to rap me on the knuckles, reminding me that 'He who grumbles at the little thing that has fallen to his lot will grumble at everything'. He warned me where that would lead – 'Always grumbling, he will lead a miserable life.' I looked around and found that what he said was true, and so stopped justifying my stupidity to myself. Then, I finally understood the impact of his words when he said: 'But the man who does his duty as he goes, putting his shoulder to the wheel, higher and higher duties will fall to his share.'

I stopped wasting energy in self-pity or thinking that I was meant for greater things. Instead, I decided to put my shoulder to the wheel, no matter what the task assigned, and left it to the inherent truth of what he said to play out in the long run.

The moment I gained the slightest relevance, however, it brought an unexpected add-on, almost instantly. One that has refused to leave my side since then: Hostility. It took the form of sharp, sustained, often bitter opposition. It was unsettling. You do not always know how to handle it. You consider walking away to give yourself a breather, but what about next month's bread and rent? And what's the assurance that situation B will be any different?

As I first faced and then got accustomed to flak, I read and re-read what the monk wrote to his disciples: 'Have faith that you are all, my brave lads, born to do great things! Let not the barks of puppies frighten you – no, not even the thunderbolts of heaven – but stand up and work!'

He explained, from his own experience, in his fiery fashion: 'The names of those who will wish to injure us will be legion. But is not that the surest sign of our having the truth? The more I have been opposed, the more my energy has always found expression.' And so, fingers crossed that the 'more I have been opposed…' rule was not for him alone, I stood up and continued to work the way it made sense to me, paying no attention to the 'disapproval of puppies' and the 'thunderbolts of heaven' alike.

That worked for upfront confrontations, but there is always more of the other kind. Slander and innuendo snake their way around and behind you and the taking-it-head-on reflex doesn't solve anything. If anything, it brings up the 'don't wrestle with a pig' caution. When I faced that first, it was both unfamiliar and disturbing. For a while, I was nostalgic about the phase of complete irrelevance – at least nobody bothered to tell tales about a nobody! Then I looked to get even. But then I realized that someone as Teflon-coated as an ordained sanyasi wasn't spared either, so what was I cribbing about? Of all people, Vivekananda's 'way of life' in the US had been questioned!

His response: 'Tell my friends that a uniform silence is all my answer to my detractors. If I give them tit for tat, it would bring me down to a level with them. Tell them that truth will take care of itself… ' I learnt that the effort to get even would mean engaging on an equal level. So, I let anyone say what they wished to – if that is what they needed for drawing a sense of fulfilment, well, to each his own. I have to assume that, in due course, the truth will take care of itself. We give too much weight to gossip. 'A uniform silence' is a tool we use far too rarely, but it has its merits; do try it.

By the time the thirties came, my body was already beginning to tire. The twenties had extracted their toll. I had stress in abundance and money had been scarce. There were days I would look despondently, wistfully, at how so many years filled with 12-hour work days had gone by, and here I was, still attempting to make something of my life. Far too many people younger than me seemed to be discussing sabbaticals and posting pictures from their endless global travelling. I would wonder whether all that rebellion was worth anything when you had little money, fame or rest well into the thirties – the only abundance was, yes, of the critics.

But Vivekananda, unforgiving teacher that he was, would still not allow self-pity to be legitimized. 'Wait,' he said, 'wait, money does not pay, nor name; fame does not pay, nor learning. It is love that pays; it is character that cleaves its way through adamantine walls of difficulties.' It was not an easy lesson to learn from him; after all, he himself had done so much and wrapped up his entire lifespan before 40. But I tried. I looked back at the most vulnerable points of my life and asked myself whether I had lasted through them because I had power or money or if it was because I stuck to a few basics. I figured out my answers, realized that money, name or fame had been utterly irrelevant in coming out in one piece from life's most complex and difficult moments – and I tried not to overrate them thereafter.

When wish after wish was unfulfilled, when 'compromise' became the default, when grand plans recurrently crashed for lack of grand resources, when I got tired of the endless waits dictated by my bank balance and lost my cool and my sense of tranquillity, I went back to him to try to curb my angst. And he told me, 'Was it ever in the history of the world that any great work was done by the rich? It is the heart and the brain that do it ever and not the purse.' Again, I did a reality check, found some sense in this, believed him and stopped assuming that my life was incapable of great things happening just because my account emptied out before each month-end.

> When I look back, the credit for whatever defiance, persistence and curiosity that still survive within goes largely to picking up Vivekananda's teachings many years ago.

Now, in my late forties, older but not much wiser, I pay house EMIs and school fees, track interest rates and cholesterol levels, attend office reviews and PTMs – essentially, live the middle-class, middle-aged life. But the mindset is still rebellious.

And when I look back, the credit for whatever defiance, persistence and curiosity that still survive within goes largely to picking up Vivekananda's teachings many years ago.

Romain Rolland wrote:

> *I cannot touch these sayings of his, scattered as they are through the pages of this book at thirty (years) distance, without receiving a thrill through my body like an electric shock. And what shock, what transport, must have been produced when, in burning words, they issued from the lips of the hero!*

Rolland wasn't exaggerating. His teachings *are* like an electric shock.

Plug in!

Part 1

Dealing with Oneself

Independence and Solitude

Decades back, when I was young, I went from being a perfectly docile, unsure child to entering a phase of rebellion, as teenagers often do.

But while most people (I assume) grow out of their teenage rebellion as they grow older, I never could. From 17 then, to 47 now, the spirit of that rebellion has refused to leave me. On the contrary, it has strengthened over the years.

Isn't that odd? Perhaps. Do I regret it? Not in the least.

My teen rebellion was never in defiance of authoritarian structures – parents, teachers, the 'system'. It was against the template of rebellion itself. That, perhaps, was the reason why it did not wane over time. My rebellion was against the hugely contradictory stereotyping of 'individuality'; against being driven by the need to be 'cool'; against the assumptions of so many things supposedly being 'obvious' because of age or gender or social placing – things which did not seem so obvious to me at all, and still don't.

As I noticed peers ostensibly seeking freedom from authority, I ended up seeking freedom from that collective quest itself. A quest that seemed to manifest itself in very similar ways in what people did, how they spoke, what they wore, what they seemed to believe in. Dozens of people doing the exact same thing at the exact same stage of life in an effort to be unique – made no sense to me.

Disengaged, if not cynical, disinterested in being cool, dismissive of what my peers thought of me, I drifted off by myself. And yet, that alone-ness did not leave me scarred for life.

Instead, I increasingly grew comfortable with being mostly by myself, without a buddy gang, without people of my age to share my joys and tears, without relating in the least to what the big deal about having friends to 'stand by you' was all about.

That comfort, that sense of not missing the approval and appreciation of people, and that too from a fairly early age when the other basics of my thinking had not yet fallen into place, I owe to Vivekananda.

There is so much fear during the growing years. We acquire so many things for the first time – self-esteem, associations, applause, understanding. As we relish the sense of acquisition, we realize it comes with a heightened fear of losing. When a friend at school who we believe 'understands' us, abruptly stops communicating because of a misunderstanding, how it trips us! The more popular we are at school, the greater the emotional void the farewell party brings. For many years of our adolescence and youth, we live on an emotional roller coaster, depending on how others feel about us, only to look back later and marvel at how those phases were so important then.

Rich cousins make us feel impoverished and inadequate. The mirror stresses us out as we obsess over how the world sees us. If we fear we do not meet those benchmarks, our confidence crumbles. It is not just the day of the Board Exam results that brings stress, there is so much more to battle in those years! And to battle it all without any 4 a.m. friends? Tragic, eh?

Not really.

In those growing years, what Vivekananda did was to put me on the route to freedom – not just from external dependence, but from my own internal deficiencies. He freed me from the need for social approval; from the need for 'safety' – emotional, financial, physical; from the need for understanding and validation from others of my age.

He filled in for my buddy gang, in a very real, very reassuring way. He gave me the freedom to be alone.

He made me absorb, over and over again, the absolute statements that he made in such a matter-of-fact manner:

I do not care a fig for human approbation or criticism.

It was so aspirational.

I was then, and still am, in many ways, especially socially, the ugly duckling who grew up into – for want of a better expression – the ugly duck. The surest way to end all joy and fun in a social gathering is to place me in some significant role in it. And so, out of compassion for my fellow humans, I usually keep a safe distance from any gathering which is about people having a good time. I cannot understand the idea of 'having a good time', cannot last half an hour at a party, cannot endure crowds, and flee loud music as quickly as it is socially acceptable without insulting anyone – and it's rather late to acquire those missing social traits now.

The reason why I made no attempt at all in all these decades to acquire them is, of course, Vivekananda.

He did not necessarily *instigate* that way of life; it was fairly deeply rooted in my introverted, reclusive, disinterested-in-the-general-universe reflexes even as a schoolboy.

What he *did* was to convince me that doing anything whatsoever to make a *deliberate* effort to be more interesting and popular, social and engaging was simply pointless; and the quest for reaching out excessively for human approval, if not human bonding, is a futile one anyway. He convinced me that I could live 'alone', as a state of mind, for most dimensions and most periods of my life, and not look at that as something which had to be 'set right'.

Essentially, Vivekananda taught – or reaffirmed – that any need for 'support' I felt was hugely overrated, and that it is possible to have very little support and yet be comfortable, stable and functional. In effect, *you* are your own support system.

Don't try too hard to seek external support – you are your own support system:

In those growing years, what Vivekananda did was to put me on the route to freedom – not just from external dependence, but from my own internal deficiencies. He filled in for my buddy gang, in a very real, very reassuring way. He gave me the freedom to be alone.

Vivekananda reaffirmed that any need for 'support' I felt was hugely overrated, and that it is possible to have very little support and yet be comfortable, stable and functional. In effect, you are your own support system. He convinced me that to make a deliberate effort to be more interesting and popular, social and engaging was pointless and that the quest for reaching out excessively for human approval, if not human bonding, is a futile one.

When I was poring over the Bhagvad Gita's basics in my earlier years, I was mightily impressed with Radhakrishnan's description of this state of existence:

> *He who discovers his true end of life and yields to it utterly is great of soul. Though everything else is taken away from him, though he has to walk the streets, cold, hungry and alone, though he may know no human being into whose eyes he can look and find understanding, he shall yet be able to go his way with a smile on his lips, for he has gained inward freedom.*

While I am not too enthralled at the idea of being cold and hungry, the other part embedded itself very early into my subconscious. This thought was fanned hugely by exposure to Vivekananda. He reminded me – in an era where selfies and Instagram didn't exist – that a life can be lived without 'caring a fig for human approbation or criticism'.

He said it, and he *lived* it. It is not that he did not have his moments of doubt. But when he did, his basics were very firm, and he had his response worked out:

> *Sometimes I become weak, being alone and struggling against odds, my God; and I think of human help. Save Thou me for ever from these weaknesses, and may I never, never seek for help from any being but Thee.*

He helped me learn how to be alone, stay alone, and be *comfortable* staying alone. That, alone, is a debt of a lifetime.

My first fortnight at an NCC camp while in college served to test all my newly gathered Vivekananda basics. As a die-hard loner, I was quite the misfit in a barracks-style existence. 'Boys will be boys', and when packed together in a camp in their college years, I realized they will be even more ribald than usual. I was unable to participate in most conversations while most fellow cadets around me were disinterested in my priorities.

I responded by picking up a book and finding an isolated spot whenever we had time on our hands. And I focused exclusively on whatever tasks we had to do. I may not have had many conversations, but by the end of the camp, I outranked, with a small pip on my shoulder, the rest of the boys in my cramped tent. I remember it vividly still: *Junior Under Officer*, the first rank of any sort I had attained in life. I had failed to win the back-slapping approval of my peers, but had, much to my surprise, won it from the officers. It was an oddly fulfilling experience. One that would repeat itself in different ways in life thereafter. It is what I now call my 'Mr Hudson moment', in the context of something Vivekananda had said. I will explain it later in the book.

A second camp some months later had another Vivekananda practical lesson for me. All my belongings were locked away in a steel trunk, tucked away in a tent and I, typically, misplaced the key. For some hours, all that I had were the clothes I was wearing. Those hours extended to a day, and then, two, as I resisted the impulse to break the lock. So, there were no books, no chocolates – none of the daily fixes that we were habituated to. Just emptiness, but curiously fulfilling. I had meals in borrowed utensils, shared sweets and snacks when there was enough to go around, and realized that I actually relished the sense of having nothing, needing nothing, even if for a very small window of time.

And in that very small lesson, I thought about the strength of what Vivekananda had said:

> *This is the one cause of misery: we are attached; we are being caught. Therefore, says the Gita, work constantly; work, but be not attached, be not caught. Reserve unto yourself the power of detaching yourself from everything, however beloved, however much the soul might yearn for it, however great the pangs of misery you feel if you are going to leave it; still, reserve the power of leaving it whenever you want.*

'Reserve unto yourself the power of detaching yourself.' – That thought and the camp's random musings came together to leave me with a reflex: to not panic if I lost the keys, and to keep testing myself occasionally if I would panic if a 'key' was lost, if something or someone precious and necessary was inaccessible. Did I have the power to detach myself even if the object was important, even precious? Was I 'caught', as Vivekananda would say?

We never try to test ourselves that way, do we? What is dear to us is assumed to be a part of our lives forever, though we know that isn't possible since we ourselves have such limited lifespans. But we avoid those topics. We rarely sit down and ask ourselves how we would react if we lost our money or our current job, or if we had to separate from someone dear to us. When our organization downsizes or when loved ones are taken away before their time, we deal with what happens with reluctance and pain. We then have no choice.

Vivekananda asks us to not react to events as they happen, but to beforehand develop the power of being able to detach ourselves from everything, 'however great the pangs of misery' we may feel about our loss. This is easier said than done, and very few of us can do it a 100 per cent. But if you keep trying, even if you can get halfway, you are, as he says, not 'caught' all the time. Every loss then does not bring us to our knees. Every change in life's status quo is not a soul-shattering blow. We are less susceptible to life's emotional blackmail, so to say.

I have tried to keep asking myself recurrently, over these decades, for most things that are important at each given point of life: Do I have the power of leaving this whenever I want? Am I 'caught' and unable to let go if needed? I may or may not leave it, but if I *need* to, will I collapse or keep walking, even if a little unsteadily?

It's a question we need to keep asking ourselves occasionally.

When, later in life, I read for the first time the story of how trappers catch monkeys by putting gram in a hollow in a tree that is just big enough for a monkey to put his hand in, but not big enough to let it pull it back after grabbing a fistful – what is called the '*bandar ki mutthi*' parable – I thought of what Vivekananda had said. The monkey reaches in, greedy to take some gram in his fist, and then realizes he cannot take the fist out without letting go. He struggles to pull his hand out. The obvious solution is to let go. But he cannot detach himself from it; he *cannot* let go. He is 'caught', as Vivekananda would say. It is a great lesson to remember. I place the monkey at one end of the emotional maturity spectrum, Vivekananda at the other, and frequently assess which extreme I am closer to. It is a great exercise in deflating the ego.

Thoughts and questions that Vivekananda forces us to engage with:

- Learning how to be alone, stay alone, and be comfortable staying alone.
- 'Reserve unto yourself the power of detaching yourself.'
- Do I have the power of leaving things whenever I want? Am I frequently 'caught' and unable to let go?

Later still, when I read about Ashoka the Great, I felt that while his rule was in itself the stuff that books have been written about, his last call as a ruler was his greatest. While I cannot vouch for the historical authenticity of various versions, the very idea that an emperor with *that* degree of power in all probability *voluntarily* relinquished the throne and walked away seemed so aspirational.

Subhas Chandra Bose is another who, twice, displayed the reflex of not being attached to things that were not easily earned. Those two sacrifices shaped his life. First, he resigned from the Indian Civil Service at a time when the ICS had power and prestige and only a handful of Indians had cracked it. And then, several years later, in a bitter stand-off with the Mahatma himself, Bose resigned as Congress president, again displaying the courage to let go. Instead, he opted to search for other ways to carry on the fight he believed in. The first resignation took him towards politics; the second one resulted in him leading the Indian National Army's effort to free India militarily.

Bose, incidentally, had read a lot of Vivekananda's writings. In the final few years of his life, he was fiercely individualistic, and it interested me greatly to observe that he worked with both the leading proponent of non-violence, Gandhi, as well as the most powerful military dictator at that point of time, Hitler, without being a disciple of either. I thought of Vivekananda's supremely confident, supremely individualistic thinking:

> *I have a mission to fulfil. I will work it out alone. I do not care who comes or who goes.*

I did not have any grand mission to fulfil, but I was still inspired enough to memorize the latter part like a cult movie line. 'I do not care who comes or who goes'. This was an incredibly difficult thought to absorb, more so by someone who was still an adolescent. I battled with it through my twenties as well, when who comes and who goes seems to be the most important thing in one's life – personally, professionally, socially. But what a brilliantly grand thought it is, if you can absorb it!

Of course, all of us do not have to step into the shoes of either Emperor Ashoka or Bose. But to reserve 'the power to let go' is significant. A 20-something putting up with an abusive relationship perhaps needs to exercise that power just as much as a CFO of a company that is fudging figures. Why are we afraid of letting go even if holding on is damaging to us?

Vivekananda is there to guide us when faced with tough choices, to remind us of the basics of freedom and independence

– to not care a fig for human approbation or criticism, to not waste energy seeking human help, to not be 'caught'. To let go.

'Loneliness does not come from having no people about one, but from being unable to communicate the things that seem important to oneself, or from holding certain views which others find inadmissible.'

Carl Gustav Jung's coherent – and accurate – description of loneliness was something that I had read, but not analysed, at about the same time as I started reading Vivekananda.

The first time I read Jung's line, long after consuming large volumes of Vivekananda, I went back to Radhakrishnan's commentary on the Gita – '*Though he may know no human being into whose eyes he can look and find understanding...*' – and understood the significance of loneliness afresh: When you can't communicate with others and there's no one to understand you, the outcome, often, is immense loneliness.

Long spells of loneliness can lead to a chronic feeling of physical isolation. But it is more about emotional than physical realities, is it not? People can spend weeks shipwrecked and alone, and reach the shore one day with their sanity intact, while others living in a building inhabited by hundreds seem to always be on the edge. Someone who seems happy living a perfectly 'normal' life may be so lonely and isolated deep down that he could slip a noose around his neck one day – and nobody would have seen it coming.

Vivekananda had made the point repeatedly and emphatically – that he did not care in the least if he was unable to communicate the things that seemed important to him. And he seemed extremely comfortable – almost flamboyantly so – holding views that others found inadmissible. On the contrary, he was usually irked by conformity.

One may safely presume, going by Jung's analysis, that he had little fear of loneliness.

That was aspirational.

Vivekananda's message was not just the typical 'believe in yourself' spiel. Over the years, I often stopped to re-read, comprehend and absorb the sheer audacity of his tone in lines like these:

- *You need not disturb yourself at all about me. I want no help from any human being in any country.*
- *You must not huddle together too many fools. I shall be glad if you bring together a few real men.*

This supremely self-contained, blunt, almost arrogant disinterest throughout his life in what people's opinions of him were, fascinated me. 'I do not care who comes or who goes' – well. What freedom that must give, if you can *actually* think that way!

While he wrote on these lines innumerable times, I found the crux of that approach in one particular letter he wrote to Mary Hale in 1895. It was like a bulldozer crashing through flimsy structures built within the mind:

- *One accommodates himself to surroundings and social opinion and gets all good things from society, the giver of all good to such. The other stands alone and draws society towards him. The accommodating man finds a path of roses; the non-accommodating one, one of thorns. But the worshippers of 'vox populi' go to annihilation in a moment; the children of truth live forever.*
- *I am so, so sorry, Sister, that I cannot make myself sweet and accommodating to every black falsehood. But I cannot. I have suffered for it all my life. But I cannot. I have essayed and essayed. But I cannot. At last I have given it up. The Lord is great. He will not allow me to become a hypocrite… I am too old to change now into milk and honey. Allow me to remain as I am.*

Whenever I have been faced with questions of 'not being understood' – and I seem to have frequently been faced with that question, usually for the worse – these incredibly unapologetic reflexes have helped me stay un-hassled. So, I've sometimes gone from 'did they really say *that* about me?' to 'is that *all* they said about me?'

No, not because I have necessarily been right always. But would I change how I did something if it left *me* uncomfortable or contrite? Probably, yes. Would I change it to earn pseudo-respect, because the local vox populi has a viewpoint on it? Probably not. There is little point in doing things differently because three people from your workspace sharing a drink in the evening may have a point of view on something about you. You could change five things you do, and they would have a point on the sixth, so meeting 50 per cent – or even 80 per cent – of their expectations wouldn't suffice to placate or pacify them. Outside of work, you could spend years trying to change the opinion of an unpleasant intrusive relative, but it is very likely that you will never meet with a 100 per cent approval. So why watch yourself all the time to just get a 40 per cent approval rating?

So, at the end of the day, what does Vivekananda's hyper-unapologetic reflex leave me with?

Essentially, this:

> *I will die a thousand deaths rather than lead a jellyfish existence and yield to every foolish requirement of this foolish world, no matter whether it be my own country or a foreign country. You are mistaken, utterly mistaken, if you think I have a work... I have no work under or beyond the sun. I have a message, and I will give it after my own fashion. I will neither Hinduise my message,*

> *nor Christianise it, nor make it any 'ise' in the world. I will only my-ise it and that is all.*

I have no grand message to give, unlike him, but as to the very small dimensions of my inconsequential, routine life, I am clear: I will, as he says, only 'my-ise it', and that is all.

Some iconic quotes by Vivekananda that shook me up while I was in my adolescence and early twenties and have stayed with me, ever since:

- I have a mission to fulfil. I will work it out alone. I do not care who comes or who goes.
- You need not disturb yourself at all about me. I want no help from any human being in any country.
- You must not huddle together too many fools. I shall be glad if you bring together a few real men.
- The worshippers of 'vox populi' go to annihilation in a moment; the children of truth live forever.
- I cannot make myself sweet and accommodating to every black falsehood.

And the most flamboyant of them all:
I will die a thousand deaths rather than lead a jellyfish existence and yield to every foolish requirement of this foolish world, no matter whether it be my own country or a foreign country ... I will neither Hinduise my message, nor Christianise it, nor make it any 'ise' in the world. I will only my-ise it and that is all.

Maybe it's not the best way to be universally popular, but now, into my forties, I can finally use that quote when someone tells me I need to be softer, more communicative, or to improve my social skills. I tell them I am too old to change now into milk and honey.

Allow me to remain as I am. And remind me to go back to this response from the monk, when in doubt, when facing flak, whether personally, professionally or socially:

> *Tell my friends that a uniform silence is all my answer to my detractors. If I give them tit for tat, it would bring us down to a level with them. Tell them that truth will take care of itself, and they are not to fight anybody for me.*

For years I've kept a print of Max Ehrmann's 'A Prayer' around my work area, and a softer, kinder version of Vivekananda's radicalized thought comes from the lines there. Ehrmann prays that:

> *Though the World knew me not, may my Thoughts and Actions be such as shall keep me friendly with Myself*

and a few lines later, requests that:

> *Let me not follow the Clamour of the World,*
> *but walk calmly in my Path*

It's a great load off the head – to not follow the clamour of the world. And, more importantly, to not regret it. Between Vivekananda and Ehrmann, therefore, I tried to learn to make peace with the world knowing me not, so long as I could keep me friendly with myself. It makes life simpler.

Fear of Loss and Death

> *'There is success and failure in every work. But I am inclined to believe that one who is a coward will after death be born as an insect or a worm, that there is no salvation for a coward even after millions of years of penance...This life is not, in my view, such a sweet thing that I would long to live through so much care and caution and fear... So loss of money, or loss of anything else – I cannot bother about, and I will not.'*
>
> *–Vivekananda*

THIS LINE OF THINKING is far more subversive of the status quo than the most extreme Marxist–Leninist ideology. 'Loss of money, or loss of anything else – I cannot bother about, and I will not.'

Seriously!

Aren't all our growing years *filled* with worrying about loss? We bother about the loss of our teachers' patronage and our class-fellows' goodwill, the loss of five marks in our exams because of a silly oversight and the loss of a little money.

When a classmate in class XII lost her eyesight, the fear of blindness shook me to the core. For a couple of hours I went around with my eyes shut to understand how it felt, leaving me even more frightened.

My understanding was that the stress over the loss of money and a hundred other things, big or small, was almost inseparable from life as we know it. Loss, and the fear of loss, is an integral part of what we are and how we live.

While Vivekananda was very clear in his thinking on loss and his response to it, for me, it was very disturbing in many ways. I couldn't even imagine that thinking like that was an option. 'I cannot bother about, and I will not' – can those of us leading everyday lives also think like that? It's all fine to *talk* like that, but beyond that...? Isn't most of our life about worrying about loss? Did we lose out on those three extra marks in the Boards? Did we miss out on getting into St. Stephen's? Did we miss out on that almost-perfect job? Did we miss out on that elusive equation with that almost-perfect someone? Did we miss a great opportunity to gain visibility at work? Did we miss making money in the share market? Will we miss catching that flight? Or even that last seat in the metro? Or the first 30 seconds of that grand online sale? Did we miss this, will we miss that...? We live most of our lives trying not to miss things, not to lose things or chances, desperately trying to hold on to what we have managed to obtain, scampering not to lose, not to miss, not to be left behind.

And then there is this clearly unrealistic man who says that this life simply isn't worth all that drama, and so he can't bother about the loss of money, or the loss of anything else. Not because he's high on dope and so cool that he can't be bothered – but because he *understands* what loss implies, and yet he won't be bothered.

Not worrying about the loss of things? How very unsettling!

And then, over time, I realized how very unconventional and very liberating this way of thinking was.

Bit by bit, as I read Vivekananda, it reinforced the basic idea that it was okay to lose things, to lose money, to lose anything, including your life. That it was okay to think about loss, to even think about death, to even prepare for it, to give up being perpetually scared. The Swami built a hierarchy within the mind, like the illustration about making a line smaller by drawing a bigger line next to it. If losing your life itself is something you try to be un-hassled about, then gaining or losing the small embellishments around that life hardly matter.

But it's not that simple, is it? Before thinking of our own death – since when *that* happens, we won't be alive to deal with it – we need to grapple with the idea of the smaller losses, since we do have to deal with them.

Vivekananda treated all loss with a sort of grand disdain. He was running out of money and was in a foreign country, a saffron-clad preacher. His critics were slandering him. His organization was collapsing. As was his health. The most serious crisis could be brought to his notice and it would be dismissed as if it were of no consequence. How did he manage that?

The crux of his thinking is perhaps this:

> *Hold your money merely as custodian for what is God's. Have no attachment for it. Let name and fame and money go; they are a terrible bondage. Feel the wonderful atmosphere of freedom!*

Not cringe at the loss of name, fame and money? He was not asking us to be magnanimous, or philosophical, when he suggested this. It was because he was saying that they were not *worth* much in the first place. So what, if we lost them? He was, on occasions, actually egging us on to let them go, for he saw them as 'a terrible bondage'.

Weeping over their loss? The thought never crossed his mind.

It is an interesting thought for us, since we are all, by reflex, trained to evaluate ourselves by how much we have gathered of things like money and fame, for they are a measure of a successful and happy life. And then we have to handle the horribly disruptive thinking of this man, who tells us that we should let money and fame go; that he who is afraid of losing honour and respect gets only disgrace; that a life full of caution and fear is just not worth living.

Of course, he understands how we feel. For, does he not say:

> *We see what a strong love men, who do not know any better, have for sense-objects, for money, dress, their wives, children, friends, and possessions. What a tremendous clinging they have to all these things!*

Of course, we have a tremendous clinging to all these things. Isn't that natural? What is he trying to say?

Perhaps the explanation is in this, a continuation of the thought process discussed earlier:

> *Our misery comes, not from work, but by our getting attached to something. Take for instance, money: money is a great thing to have, earn it, says Krishna; struggle hard to get money, but don't get attached to it. So with children, with wife, husband, relatives, fame, everything; you have no need to shun them, only don't get attached.*

He does not ask us to wear saffron robes and shun money, or fame, or our kin. But he does ask us to not be *obsessed* with earning money, retaining honour – for what is it but the opinion of others? And on 'owning' our friends, family, children: the more our obsession with them, the less our ability to deal with their loss.

There is so much that you cannot control. The stock market can crash and wipe out half of your savings; a smear campaign against you can mar your impeccable reputation; your spouse can choose to dump you and prefer to live happily ever after with someone else. Do you really need to lock yourself in a room and feel that the world has collapsed when misfortune knocks on your door?

You could, perhaps, read what Vivekananda has said on this and gain another perspective on the situation.

Be not *attached*. Much of what you think is the core of your life is just a 'terrible bondage'. If it goes – let it go!

Personally, I managed to live through a lot of unpleasant times by reminding myself of these basics. If money wasn't much to begin with, and what little was there got spent in handling assorted emergencies through the twenties and thirties, it irked a bit, but it didn't trip me, for, influenced by Vivekananda's contempt for money, I never saw more cash in the bank as greater 'security'. I also learnt that the only way to be never at the risk of your 'honour' being questioned was to be in a corner and do nothing at all. After a point, I preferred the inevitability of the occasional 'loss of fame' to vegetating irrelevantly in a safe zone.

It is the lesser of the two evils.

And then there is this note, which has stayed on my table for at least twenty years and has served as a reference point over and over:

> *This I have seen in life – he who is over-cautious about himself, falls into dangers at every step; he who is afraid of losing honour and respect, gets only disgrace; he who is afraid of loss, always loses.*

When Vivekananda spoke of 'he who is afraid of losing honour and respect, gets only disgrace', he cut the umbilical cord that equates success and well-being to what other people think of us. If you actually manage to be not afraid of losing honour and respect, you're slicing through your middle-class veins in one sharp stroke. For isn't that what we always live in dread of? From the neighbourhood aunt to the grocer to the

Loss is inevitable – learn to not overrate it to make it bigger than it is:

- In class XII, a classmate lost her eyesight and the fear of blindness shook me to the core. I understood that loss and the fear of it, is an integral part of what we are and how we live.
- Bit by bit, as I read Vivekananda's writings, they reinforced the basic idea that it was okay to lose things, money, even your life. That it was okay to think about loss, to even think about death, to even prepare for it, to give up being scared.
- But it's not that simple, is it? Before thinking of our own death – since when that happens, we won't be alive to deal with it – we need to grapple with the idea of the smaller losses, since we do have to deal with them.
- Vivekananda treated all loss with a sort of grand disdain. Finally, I understood what lay behind his thinking in these quotes: 'Hold your money merely as custodian for what is God's. Have no attachment for it. Let name and fame and money go; they are a terrible bondage. Feel the wonderful atmosphere of freedom!'

  'Our misery comes, not from work, but by our getting attached to something. Take for instance, money: money is a great thing to have, earn it, says Krishna; struggle hard to get money, but don't get attached to it. So with children, with wife, husband, relatives, fame, everything; you have no need to shun them, only don't get attached.'
- He does not ask us to wear saffron robes and shun money, or fame, or our kin. But he asks us to not be obsessed with earning money. The more our obsession with them, the less our ability to deal with their loss. 'Much of what you think is the core of your life is just a terrible bondage.' If it goes – let it go!
- When you absorb what he is saying, you end up building a sort of comfort level with the idea of loss. It affects, but doesn't overwhelm, and you live in less fear.

guard at the residential society's gate to the colleague in the cubicle opposite yours – we are obsessed by what others think about us. Our dressing, our behaviour, our choices are always significantly impacted by the need to meet with approval, or at least to not meet with disapproval.

Vivekananda's thought track leads to a standalone trail in most things you do, a detachment from what people think of you, a comfort level with the absence of support groups. If life were Facebook, that track of thought could be described as not being interested either in expanding your friends' list, or in posting anything primarily driven by the need for it to be liked.

When he asks us to just live our lives and not be constantly afraid of losing honour and respect, since that defensive, politically correct, timid model of living is more likely to earn us disdain than anything else in the long run, it's as close to a case of social sedition as it can get.

After the first subversive lesson, of not bothering about what is gained and what is lost, this was even more unsettling. This is such a key point that even though you've just read it, I want to repeat it:

> *This I have seen in life – he who is over-cautious about himself, falls into dangers at every step; he who is afraid of losing honour and respect, gets only disgrace; he who is afraid of loss, always loses.*

Essentially, the *more* you are prone to conserving, protecting, holding close, the more likely you are to *actually* lose whatever it is that you're grasping. And not just tangibles like money or property or jobs. What little interest I had in the viewpoints or opinions of Tom, Dick and Harry faded away once I had absorbed the crux of 'he who is afraid of losing honour and respect...' What little attention I used to pay to caution and carefulness, for want of a better word, atrophied and faded over time as 'he who is over-cautious…' made its way into the system.

Whatever other vices and deficiencies I have continued to carry with me, Vivekananda rooted out most of my childhood timidity.

Every few days or weeks or months, something would stick in my mind, would be marked, highlighted, circled, then a print taken, tacked up, dissected, debated, but most often, absorbed. Even if he was often addressing fellow-monks, even if it was *all* addressed to men in saffron robes, the sheer romanticism, the audacity of the thoughts such as this would draw me to them:

> *Whenever you think of yourself, you are bound to feel restless. What business have you to do with peace, my boy?*

But whatever else I marked and made notes around, whatever else engaged me on a given day, I would keep coming back to that earlier line, the one that delivered such a nasty knock to the foundation of all the status quo-centric salaried-class basics I would have otherwise unthinkingly absorbed – 'This life is not, in my view, such a sweet thing that I would long to live through so much care and caution and fear...'

At the larger level, I observed that the obsession with building and preserving our little kingdoms of money, fame and assorted add-ons was, for want of a better word, essentially middle-class. Wasn't it? Large corporations seem to gain or lose millions on a given day as stocks fluctuate, but nobody has a heart attack. I read about war and was amazed at how German and Soviet generals traded hundreds of miles and thousands of men as they played out their moves on the killing grounds of WWII. I read about an Allied general, reading *War and Peace* before an upcoming battle, commenting to a colleague about Kutuzov: 'He's the kind of General to study. He knew that in war, steadiness and endurance are more important than any amount of strategic flair.'

As Vivekananda said, 'there is success and failure in every work'. We can't control what happens, we can't always control what we lose – money, fame, a relationship that meant the world to us. Or a World Cup final. What we can control is how we react to the loss.

Perhaps what Vivekananda is suggesting is not just a detached monk's world view, after all. Tycoons have lost billions, and generals have lost entire armies, political leaders have been exiled and lost their countries – yet not all of them necessarily react by worrying or collapsing. 'The loss of anything' – they have not bothered about excessively. The New Zealand cricket team gained worldwide respect for how it absorbed a heartbreakingly unfair 'loss' to England in the 2019 World Cup finals. Many other teams and fans would have been swept away in despair or hysteria.

As Vivekananda said, 'there is success and failure in every work'. We can't control what happens, we can't always control what we lose – money, fame, a relationship that meant the world to us. Or a World Cup final. What we can control is how we react to the loss. And how would Vivekananda have us react to it? By affirming that the 'loss of money, or loss of *anything* else I cannot bother about, and I will not'.

Death – I

NOW, WE COME TO the great leveller – death. In most things, we may well discount the relevance of a monk's basics in our more 'worldly' and 'practical' lives, but at this point our paths converge. Philosopher or junkie, austere or debauch, super successful or pavement-dweller – death will come to all of us, and each one of us will have to handle it individually. No matter how plush the ICU ward is or how many relatives are surrounding the bed, if you feel you have only a few gasps of breath remaining, it is highly unlikely that the number of Facebook or Instagram likes you got for all your philosophical ramblings and your exotic vacations will matter.

Death engaged me as a topic in my teens, as I guess it does most young people, and then after a while, I attempted to leave it as a problem to be resolved at a later point of time. However, it kept coming back, like a jumbled Rubik's cube in front of me on the study table. You can't help thinking of solutions. To a degree, perhaps, it was accelerated by several road accidents over the years, and the sense of 'Oops, I could have died right here!' Life has a very different perspective as you are flying off a hilly highway for 20-odd metres before landing on your head, or when you are lying knocked down on the road, vaguely noticing that the headlights and tyres heading your way are that of a roadways bus which seems to be making only a rather half-hearted attempt to hold on to the tarmac so as to not make contact with your face. Yes, a lot of thoughts *do* flash through your mind when you think you're going to die.

Death manages to scare us both ways, paradoxically. While one fear is of an untimely death, another is of a painful, helplessly prolonged life. I have often thought that it is important for me to have a few friends whom I can call upon to do what the coach did for his ward in *Million Dollar Baby* – in that situation, death is infinitely less scary than a helpless existence. More so after seeing the lives of names that were rock stars to me, from a Christopher Reeve to a Michael Schumacher, transform in a few moments.

Vivekananda did not give me an answer to my constantly changing queries on life and death, but he did give a sense of perspective:

> *We always forget that this world is a means to an end, and not an end itself. If this were the end we should be immortal here in our physical body; we should never die. But we see people every moment dying around us, and yet, foolishly, we think we shall never die; and from that conviction we come to think that this life is the goal. That is the case with ninety-nine per cent of us. This notion should be given up at once. This world is good so far as it is a means to perfect ourselves; and as soon as it has ceased to be so, it is evil.*

This is an interesting thought. And like almost all of what he would say, disruptive. We are trained to always wish people 'many, many happy returns of the day', we read news reports on the world's oldest person cutting a cake amidst much fanfare, and so on – essentially the longer the body stays here, the happier it is for the individual. Vivekananda, however, says that to think that 'this life is the goal' is an error in itself. And if it is *not* the goal, what great difference does it make whether we spend 45 or 90 rounds of the sun here?

I was once having a conversation with a cinematic celebrity, something that my job occasionally needs me to do.

Not only was he in the Bentley-driving league, but his lineage was as illustrious as the vehicles he drove and the watches he sported. He was then in his thirties. In the context of something he had recently done, I asked him a question that had often engaged my mind.

My query was roughly this: 'In normal middle-class India, we get rebuked for even talking about death. If we attend a cremation, we come back and take a bath immediately, to wash the vibes of the cremation ground off us. I don't think any of us will experience lying on a pyre at a cremation ground till we have passed the point of experiencing anything. You recently shot scenes X and Y – only actors get to do that – where you lie on a stretcher, covered with a sheet, and are carried by four men holding it up; finally, you actually lie on the wood piled up at a cremation ground. I can only ask an actor if those moments made you think of how the *actual* journey will be. Did you think about when all this acting will be replayed as reality? Does the experience of the last journey make you think about how life has been, how you will handle the end when it approaches?'

The illustrious star continued to munch on his samosa while I finished explaining what I was trying to ask, then dipped the last piece in sauce with a great deal of gravitas, the sort that is there when the mind is deeply processing something. And then, with an 'I'm too young to think about these things,' he popped the surviving saucy bit of samosa into his mouth. That was the end of the topic. A one-line answer to my 10-line question.

I had been envious of him, for those experiences of having a dummy run of the last journey, but I came away realizing that everyone takes away very different things from identical experiences. The point of being 'too young' echoed for many days. I wondered if I was in need of counselling. I had been thinking about death since I was in school.

Somewhere from that line of thought, possibly, I got back to reading about how Vivekananda thought a lot about his own death and seemed to be prepared for it much in advance.

In a letter written in July 1897, Vivekananda actually spelt out a timeline for what he felt was a reverse countdown commencing: 'I feel my task is done – at most three or four years more of life are left.' Three years later, in a letter to Sister Nivedita in March 1900, he wrote:

> *I don't want to work. I want to be quiet, and rest. I know the time and the place; but the fate, or Karma, I think, drives me on – work, work.*

In my fraying, torn, massively underlined and marked copy of *Letters of Swami Vivekananda*, I'd marked, 'I know the time and place' the very first time I read and pondered over it, and made a small note against it: 'of death, obviously.' I could find no other explanation. About five years after talking of 'three or four years of life', just over two years after writing that letter to Sister Nivedita, Vivekananda died, on 4 July 1902, after conducting a detailed study of the almanac in the preceding days, specifically pointing out the spot of his cremation three days before his moving on, and issuing detailed instructions to brother-disciples on the future of the Ramakrishna Math on the day of his death itself. Romain Rolland has noted that Vivekananda began to decline to express his opinion on the questions of the day earlier in that year itself with the response, 'I can no more enter into outside affairs; I am already on the way.' He had said, years in advance:

> *I shall not live to be forty years old.*

Clearly, he was no stranger to the wrapping up of his time here, and approached it with a sense of anticipation, if not a comfortable familiarity.

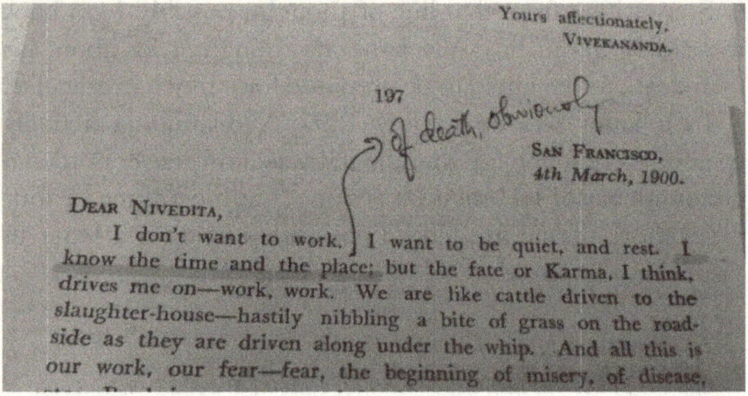

Yours affectionately,
VIVEKANANDA.

197

SAN FRANCISCO,
4th March, 1900.

DEAR NIVEDITA,

I don't want to work. I want to be quiet, and rest. I know the time and the place; but the fate or Karma, I think, drives me on—work, work. We are like cattle driven to the *slaughter-house*—hastily nibbling a bite of grass on the road-side as they are driven along under the whip. And all this is our work, our fear—fear, the beginning of misery, of disease,

I'd often thought how evolved a mind had to be, to sense when time here is going to run out, and yet, to go on with a sense of energy, and a purpose of a mission to be accomplished before time runs out. Over the years since I read it, I mused that perhaps it was the other way round – perhaps the very fact of knowing 'the time and the place' could have made his life driven the way it was: No time to waste, knowing the clock is ticking away.

The more I thought about it, the more it taught me that there is a manner of living which is free of the hysterical fear of death that inhibits our everyday lives, where just the mention of the 'inauspicious' word draws reprimand.

The trucker's philosophy of life, that we follow so often while driving on hilly roads where there is little scope to overtake for miles, is '*Bhagwaan aur maut ko hamesha yaad rakho*'. (Never forget God and death.) Vivekananda never forgot God, given the life he led, but he never forgot death either. He understood early in life that they were both certainties, interwoven and inseparable.

There are ways to talk about and to approach death, without panic, with grace:

- We may not be able to emulate Vivekananda's life. Yet, his gentle, even friendly, embrace of death gives us much to absorb and think about. His life reminds us that death can be faced without fear or panic, without a sense of despair or loss.
- Vivekananda never forgot God, given the life he led, but he never forgot death either. He understood early in life that they were both certainties, interwoven and inseparable.

We may not be able to emulate his life. Yet, his gentle, even friendly, embrace of death gives us much to absorb and think about. His life reminds us that death can be faced without fear or panic, without a sense of despair or loss. His foreknowledge of it shows us that even a man who can see his final day approaching can continue to go about his daily duties with vigour. He leaves us with the hope that if we are able to work on ourselves, we, too, can perhaps at least have a faint sense of when our time is approaching, and calmly accept that with grace.

The closer our lives are to his, is it not feasible that the closer the manner of our death could be, too? Following his thinking, we could lead a life that is somewhat philosophical and not excessively possessive, to help us make it easier to head towards the final gate less painfully and frantically. Will greater dignity and gravitas in life assure us of a less hysterical disengagement when we finally realize time is running out?

Possibly.

Should we also not stop seeing conversations about death as inauspicious or depressing? Do we need to hurry to change the topic when the possibility of our death, or of someone who matters to us, is even accidentally brought up? Even our life insurance advertising is so sanitized that you barely get a sense that it prepares your kin for living after your death.

And it is this thought that tells me why reading and absorbing the sense of Vivekananda's death is a fulfilling, important exercise. It is my emotional 'life insurance'. I invest in it while I am living and build up that fund, that reservoir that I can tap into at the end, hopefully. Except that, in this case, I am both the depositor and the beneficiary.

Death – II

NO MATTER WHAT WE read and absorb, doesn't the fear of death – the fear of leaving everything and everyone behind – follow us all the time? Frankly, I have a greater fear of the *manner* of death – the way in which one leaves behind the body – than of the fact of it. I once read a story about an old lady who said she wasn't afraid of death, but of *dying* – that she was very secure about being taken care of by God in the afterlife, but worried if her final years would be confined to a bed, with tubes and needles, if she would be in pain, if she would still be able to recognize those she loved.

I thought this was a very simple but profound distinction – the fear of death and the fear of dying as two separate things. You can be not so scared about the former and yet be petrified of the latter.

Which is perhaps why I have been awestruck by the way Vivekananda left his body. But we have spoken of that already.

What exactly are we afraid of, though? Vivekananda is there to nudge us to the topic and to remind us, if only we let him, that:

> *The whole world is going towards death; everything dies. All our progress, our vanities, our reforms, our luxuries, our wealth, our knowledge, have that one end — death. That is all that is certain. Cities come and go, empires rise and fall, planets break into pieces and crumble into dust, to be blown about by the atmospheres of other planets. Thus, it has been going on from time without beginning.*

Death is the end of everything. Death is the end of life, of beauty, of wealth, of power, of virtue too. Saints die and sinners die, kings die and beggars die. They are all going to death, and yet this tremendous clinging on to life exists. Somehow, we do not know why, we cling to life; we cannot give it up. And this is Maya.

Do we, after all these years, still experience this? This tremendous clinging to life?

Of course, we do.

So we live in dread of what we cannot avoid or escape, something that is written for us the very day we are born. How will we, then, not live in fear? Is the only other choice to live in delusion?

Death is stalking day and night over this earth of ours, but at the same time we think we shall live eternally. A question was once asked of King Yudhishthira, 'What is the most wonderful thing on this earth?' And the king replied, 'Every day, people are dying around us, and yet men think they will never die.' And this is Maya.

We have all heard the story of Yudhishthira and the Yaksha, of course. But there is more that Vivekananda has to say on it:

Great men have died. Weak men have died. Gods have died. Death — death everywhere. This world is a graveyard of the infinite past, yet we cling to this [body]: 'I am never going to die.' Knowing for sure [that the body must die] and yet clinging to it. There is meaning in that too [because in a sense we do not die]. The mistake is that we cling to the body when it is the spirit that is really immortal.

Vivekananda asks us to renounce the body. He reiterates what the Gita has told us, but, of course, with his added flamboyance:

> *I am the spirit — the soul no instrument can pierce, no sword can cut asunder, no fire can burn, no air can dry. Unborn and uncreated, without beginning and without end, deathless, birthless and omnipresent — that is what I am; and all misery comes just because I think this little lump of clay is myself. I am identifying myself with matter and taking all the consequences.*

'All misery comes because I think this little lump of clay is myself.'

I thought of this when I first heard, in the film *Peepli Live*, the beautifully crafted lyrics by the folk poet Ganga Ram Siware, sung soulfully by Nageen Tanvir:

> *Chola maati ke Ram,*
> *Ekar ka bharosa, chola maati ke re.*

It is soothing to listen to, and makes you pause and reflect.

A literal translation deprives it of the feel, but the core thought is that the human body is a 'chola' (robe/garment) made of 'maati' (clay): *this little lump of clay*.

With this line of thought, Vivekananda also pauses your default thinking that regards caring for the body as the core of religion, that equates financial charity, welfare and social support as the sum total of spiritual growth. One can lead to the other, for sure, but they are not quite the same. He says to us:

> *Practical religion is identifying myself with my Self. Stop this wrong identification! How far are you advanced in that? You may have built two thousand hospitals, built fifty thousand roads, and yet what of that, if you, have not realised that you are the spirit? You die a dog's death, with the same feelings that the dog does. The dog howls and weeps because he knows that he is only matter and he is going to be dissolved.*

Now, this may be a tad simplistic, in the context of thc last line, because in many situations and cases, we see that animals embrace death, especially when it comes as a result of disease or ageing, with perhaps more calmness and a greater sense of acceptance than the human mind.

But that is nitpicking. I understand the point of what Vivekananda is saying to us. That the things we do to make our lives better don't answer, very often, the basic questions of where we go after death. It is a decent, noble thing to build hospitals, roads, schools, and do all that we can to make our lives here more sustainable, kinder and easier, especially for the disadvantaged. But the sense of goodness or religiousness that we get from such deeds will still not be sufficient for us to understand the larger reality of life and death. Once we have mastered the basics of sustaining and caring for physical life, it is time to try to, as Vivekananda says, stop identifying ourselves with the lump of clay. As Maslow's hierarchy of needs reminds us, once the basic, lower needs are fulfilled, the need for self-actualization should kick in.

And this won't happen with reading philosophical or religious texts just for the sake of reading – for bookish knowledge will seldom help us handle actual challenges. Everyone can put a quote on death on social media, but let that not give us the illusion that we are prepared for the moment we *actually* come face to face with death, please. The search is to genuinely believe, understand and realize that:

> *There is death, you know, inevitable death, in water, in air, in the palace, in the prison — death everywhere. What makes you fearless? When you have realized what you are — that infinite spirit, deathless, birthless. Him no fire can burn, no instrument kill, no poison hurt. Not theory, mind you. Not reading books. . . . [Not parroting.] My old Master used to say, 'It is all very good to teach the parrot to say, "Lord, Lord, Lord" all the time; but let the cat come and take hold of*

> *its neck, it forgets all about it.' [You may] pray all the time, read all the scriptures in the world, and worship all the gods there are, [but] unless you realise the soul there is no freedom. Not talking, theorizing, argumentation, but realisation. That I call practical religion.*

What is Vivekananda telling us?

He is explaining that we *cannot* understand, handle, absorb or accept death the way we ideally should – knowing and understanding that we are more than the physical body, more than a lump of clay – unless we realize the basics.

He observes that we may pray all the time, read all the scriptures in the world, worship all the gods there are – to which I must add, you could forward all the religious messages on WhatsApp on all holy days, send many vibrant emojis as reactions, fast all you can, attend all the religious gatherings you are invited to – but despite all that, there is still no freedom, *genuine* freedom, unless the soul is realized. You may have liked a thousand messages on WhatsApp, watched a thousand YouTube videos by different religious gurus, and kept a hundred fasts, and yet, on the day you realize is probably going to be your last, you may be just as clueless and panicked as someone who has done none of that.

To repeat Vivekananda's words: 'Not talking, theorising, argumentation, but realisation. That I call practical religion.'

Can we realize? Can we remember that this lump of clay is not us? Can we not, as he says, not 'cling to the body' mentally and emotionally? Can we not wait for moments of fear and gut-wrenching pain to question what comes after death? Can we not search for the answer in advance and not on the day of the exam? Can we not be fearful of our own, inevitable, ever-approaching death?

Getting to that stage, to me, is, what Vivekananda calls 'practical religion'. We can get there. We *must* get there.

Else, the fear always hovers around and catches us at a moment's notice.

When Vivekananda says that 'the mistake is that we cling to the body', he reminds me of a footnote Radhakrishnan added to his commentary on the Gita. Those short lines have brought me some calm and composure when I have thought of the moment when my time will be over.

Crito: In what way shall we bury you, Socrates?
Socrates: In any way you like, but first, you must catch me, the real me. Be of good cheer, my dear Crito, and say that you are burying my body only, and do with that whatever is usual and what you think best.

I remember laughing the first time I read this. How does a man who is to drink a cup of hemlock – execution by poisoning, in effect – have the mental capacity to be so lucid and clear? Does he not, with this approach, take away all the fear we associate with the loss of the body?

There is a certain quiet elegance to this that resonates with me. It is something I would like to say to those who care for me, who may perhaps miss my existence when I would be no more: 'Be of good cheer, and with my frail, tired, worn-out body, do whatever is usual. But do remember, that is not me. Try to catch the *real* me – not that many would want to, but still, know that only the body has gone, not me.'

Yes, my own body probably won't be buried, but burying, cremating, whatever it is, is of little consequence – we obsess too much about the rituals, thinking that they are the core of our faith, religion and culture whereas what we *should* be obsessing about is what lies beyond, where we go and where we have come from.

'I have bundled my things and am waiting for the great deliverer'

I want to share one more thing with you while we are on this subject.

There is a very intense, very heartfelt letter that Vivekananda wrote in 1900. I realize now that I have begun to turn to it when I have thoughts of my mortality or when life just tires me out, given how ill-equipped I am for the hustle, struggles and the constant conflict that seem to be a precondition for all aspects of life today – practical, professional, emotional.

Vivekananda, in his letter, sounds tired – or maybe 'exhausted' is the right word – of organizational matters, and personal debates and conflict.

He then goes into an emotional, philosophical tone that is both fatalistic and calming at the same time. Out of all the letters in *Letters of Swami Vivekananda*, I found this one to be among the most poignant, sentimental and comforting.

Read these lines for yourself and try to visualize the headspace of the person writing this:

I am well, very well mentally. I feel the rest of the soul more shall that of the body. The battles are lost and won, I have bundled my things and am waiting for the great deliverer.

'Shiva, O Shiva, carry my boat to the other shore.'

After all, Joe, I am only the boy who used to listen with rapt wonderment to the wonderful words of Ramakrishna under the Banyan at Dakshineswar. That is my true nature; works and activities, doing good and so forth are all superimpositions. Now I again hear his voice; the same old voice thrilling my soul. Bonds are breaking — love dying, work becoming tasteless — the glamour is off life. Only the voice of the Master calling. — 'I come Lord, I come.' 'Let the dead bury the dead, follow thou Me.' — 'I come, my beloved Lord, I come.'

Yes, I come. Nirvana is before me. I feel it at times — the same infinite ocean of peace, without a ripple, a breath.

I am glad I was born, glad I suffered so, glad I did make big blunders, glad to enter peace. I leave none bound, I take no bonds. Whether this body will fall and release me or I enter into freedom in the body, the old man is gone, gone for ever, never to come back again!

give them all my love and gratitude.

I am well, very well mentally. I feel the rest of the soul more than that of the body. The battles are lost and won. I have bundled my things and am waiting for the great deliverer.

"Shiva, O Shiva, carry my boat to the other shore."

After all, Joe, I am only the boy who used to listen with rapt wonderment to the wonderful words of Ramakrishna under the Banyan at Dakshineswar. That is my true nature; work and activities, doing good and so forth are all superimpositions. Now I again hear his voice; the same old voice thrilling my soul. Bonds are breaking—love dying, work becoming tasteless—the glamour is off life. Now only the voice of the Master calling. —"I come Lord, I come,"— "Let the dead bury the dead, follow thou Me." "I come, my beloved Lord, I come."

Yes, I come. Nirvâna is before me. I feel it at times—the same infinite ocean of peace, without a ripple, a breath.

I have often quietly marvelled at these thoughts, these sentiments: 'The battles are lost and won, I have bundled my things and am waiting for the great deliverer.'

Imagine that. To look forward to the wrapping up of life, not with fear and despair or as being dragged away, but to look up to Him and say: 'I have done what I had to, I seek nothing more here. I have bundled up my things and am waiting for you. Take me when you will.'

This is not the fear of death. Neither is this frustration with life and a desperation to end it all. No. It is calm, warm, deep acceptance and trust in the powers above.

Of course, when we reach the end of our days on Earth, to see life the way Vivekananda did, we have to *live* and *think* a bit like him. If we have identified only with our investments, cars, social reach and medical reports all our lives, this reflex may be rather unnatural. In being very practical and leading what we see as 'successful' lives, we sometimes miss the ability to trust in the great deliverer. Even if we think we are very 'religious', by focusing more on rituals than genuine understanding, by viewing our faith merely as a means to an end – asking God for better health, money or status – we extend our roots so deeply into the Earth's soil that leaving it seems scary.

Bonds are breaking — love dying, work becoming tasteless — the glamour is off life.

The above thought, to me, is not sad. It is, if anything, romantic, in a Guru Dutt-esque way, is it not? 'The glamour is off life' … *'Yeh duniya agar mil bhi jaaye to kya hai?'*, right?

It also makes me think of what Vivekananda wrote in another letter. This is another thought of his that I connect strongly with:

This life is not, in my view, such a sweet thing that I would long to live through so much care and caution and fear.

I feel that way from time to time, too – that the world isn't as sweet, that the 'glamour is' slowly 'off life'.

And now I don't see it as something that needs correcting, something that needs me to consult a therapist. I see it as a reminder that ultimately, very little of the work and bonds here – whatever consumes our time and energy – will stay with me in the journey ahead, beyond physical existence.

This planet is not that aspirational a place to stay on forever. Being obsessed with our work and bonds here is one way to live, but it is not the *only* way to live. Yes, live in the world till time permits, but maybe you can live more freely once you are not so awestruck with worldly things like financial status, personal charm, a good physique, etc., once 'the glamour is off life'? At some point, we should perhaps outgrow the hooks and our addiction to the drama that life brings us, and begin to 'bundle' our 'things'.

I'll conclude with these lines from the same letter:

Behind my work was ambition, behind my love was personality, behind my purity was fear, behind my guidance the thirst of power! Now they are vanishing, and I drift. I come! Mother, I come! In Thy warm bosom, floating wheresoever Thou takest me, in the voiceless, in the strange, in the wonderland, I come — a spectator, no more an actor.

Oh, it is so calm! My thoughts seem to come from a great, great distance in the interior of my own heart. They seem like faint, distant whispers, and peace is upon everything, sweet, sweet peace — like that one feels for a few moments just before falling into sleep, when things are seen and felt like shadows — without fear, without love, without emotion. Peace that one feels alone, surrounded with statues and pictures — I come! Lord, I come!

'Without fear, without love, without emotion.'

How inspirational, how peaceful, how tranquil, to be able to look towards the end like that. How aspirational, indeed, to accept, even welcome – instead of panicking, fretting and looking in the other direction – the final journey and to say with a clear conscience, 'I come!'

To be able to say *that*, to me, is life's ultimate mic drop moment.

Spirituality, Religion, Faith

'There is only one purpose in the whole of life – education. Otherwise what is the use of men and women, land and wealth?'

– Vivekananda

VIVEKANANDA GAVE ME A vague sense of what religion in general, and Hinduism in particular, was. More importantly, he gave me a sharp sense of what it was *not*, thus helping me to keep away from much of the default interpretations of it and to explore my own version – an exploration that is still a work in progress.

After three decades or so of absorbing him, I still cannot lecture anyone on what religion is, or what the faith I was born into is all about. I did not study him or Hinduism as a scholar. But I absorbed enough of the essence of what he was saying to know when to turn away when I was being fed less genuine versions by self-declared experts. I refuse to acknowledge any 'teacher' as superior to him on this topic – at least anyone born in the last few hundred years. Ramakrishna the practitioner and Vivekananda the messenger have, to me, been more than sufficient to answer the questions of a lifetime.

Thanks to Vivekananda, I have been comfortable being only half-aware of the answers to most questions on such matters. I have also been acutely aware that I am only half-aware, and have thereby hopefully escaped the mistaken arrogance of certainty that 'knowledge' of religion can bring upon us.

I deliberately stayed away from a huge part of Vivekananda's scholarly work on religion, because I had neither the experience nor the intellect to analyse it. He spoke extensively on the Vedas and Vedanta, the Atman and death, Maya and illusion, Raja Yoga and Bhakti Yoga, society and evolution, Christ and Buddha, and on a thousand other subjects. I did not delve into those, since I was not on a quest to decipher the mysteries of existence.

Unlike him, the only person I had to teach was myself.

My goals were limited to getting a sense of what the bigger picture is – to understand if there's any direction to our living at all. In my early years, I was caught in a zone of discomfort: there was a tendency for people more qualified to tell me what deity to worship, what day to fast on, what hand to use for what ritual, and so on. While understanding that they must have a rationale for all this, that faith is not necessarily blind, I still chafed at being *instructed* – it was like being forced to take classes in a subject without being explained the core of that subject.

Vivekananda, in his casual, candid, outrageous and, very often, humorous take on issues, enabled me to acquire a comfort level and then prodded me to follow a few topics in greater detail. Without having to choose between either being an atheist or blindly embracing all that I was taught without question, I could, in my own awkward, hesitating way, be 'religious', and explore things for myself.

When I was 12, I proudly declared myself to be 'not religious', an atheist. It took me some time to understand that what the 12-year-old actually meant was that, a) he didn't understand enough to even have an opinion on if he believed in God, life after death, and such concepts, and b) he definitely had no inkling of what being 'religious' was – or how to pray, what to pray for, when to fast, and where to head for a pilgrimage.

As I grew up a bit, I wavered on the 'atheist' part because it made no sense that being born and dying should be so random and of no great consequence. I also could not fully buy into the 'you only live once', so 'live it up', 'get a taste of everything' school of thought, for it seemed too bohemian for me to relate to.

I, therefore, could not grow into a dedicated non-believer, for I had too many questions that did not have obvious answers.

On the other hand, ritualism irked me and associates, relatives and the few 'holy men' I chanced upon – a priest who had come to perform a puja at home, another one at a temple, a flamboyant looking sadhu at Haridwar – were often unable to answer my random queries with enough conviction. I had far too many unresolved questions.

Given my scepticism and lack of satisfactory answers to my numerous queries on God and religion, I could not grow into a dedicated, God-fearing 'religious' believer either.

Fortunately, Vivekananda pulled me out from that ideological no-man's-land and taught me that I could continue to be in *neither* of those zones and yet have some degree of clarity on what life was about. Or at least on what path to explore if I wanted greater clarity.

What little I learnt from him over these years can be summed up in these core lessons:

1. There *is* something – call Him (or Her) what you will. It's not just a cosmic accident.
2. The rituals, customs, books, are all aids to religion – but they are *not* religion.
3. Criticize no one, for all doctrines and creeds have some good in them.
4. We know very little. Place your trust beyond the intellect.

Lesson 1: There is a greater purpose, entity, power – call Him, or Her, what you will

Spending time with the thoughts of Vivekananda leaves you with the dissatisfied sense that living isn't just about getting through school and college, getting a job, having a family, a house, and finally, some years later, waiting for life support to be pulled off from you in an ICU. It is not a pointless, accidental existence. There is more to life. There is life beyond death, there is karma, and there is far more to existence than our eyes can see or our ears can hear. There is rationality beyond our minds. People have applied their minds to these matters for thousands of years. But Vivekananda is among the better researchers worth paying attention to and a good guide to navigate you through a complex maze.

A guide blessed by an incredible guide himself.

Narendra to Ramakrishna: Sir, have you seen God?

Ramakrishna: Yes, I have seen God. I have seen Him more tangibly than I see you.

What more direct conversation can you have on this topic?

Vivekananda began with asking Ramakrishna this, and ended with a similar experience, two days before Ramakrishna's passing, when he wondered, as he stood beside the bed of his critically ill master, whether he was really an incarnation of God. And then Ramakrishna, lying on the bed, slowly uttered: 'He who in the past was born as Rama and Krishna is now living in this very body as Ramakrishna – and not just from the standpoint of your Vedanta!'

This would have been an incredibly challenging journey as a student. From the man who would be your master saying to you, matter-of-factly, that he had seen God, to that master on his deathbed reading your thoughts and saying to you, essentially, that not only was he an avatar right now, he had been so in previous lives as well.

In the frame of just these two episodes, there are questions that can take decades for the mind to handle. But if you trust Vivekananda's coherence and sanity, you can no longer think of these things as philosophy, mythology or theory.

It is *reality*.

The question no longer is *if* there is a greater entity. The question is how do we get to a point where *we* can ask such questions and get such answers.

Across hundreds of his speeches, letters and conversations over time, Vivekananda takes the point for granted and his absolute belief rubs off on you, eliminating the cynicism that the intellect loves to bring in:

> *I am sorry to see in the West how much they make of death: always trying to catch a little life. 'Give us life after death! Give us life!' they are so happy if anybody tells them that they are going to live afterwards! How can I ever doubt such a thing! ... The idea of immortality is inherent in man. How can one discuss a subject that is unimaginable?*

He never doubted once he had clarity, even though he doubted hugely before he gained it. Over and over, he drilled into you, the basics.

> *Am I, then, nothing but a combination of material substances? The Vedas declare 'No'. I am a spirit living in a body. I am not the body. The body will die, but I shall not die. Here am I in this body; it will fall, but I will go on living. I had also a past.*

If you, by force of habit, went back into the frame of the daily grind where bread and butter issues are foremost, he was there to reprimand you in less than gentle words:

> *To think that this world is the aim and end of life is brutal and degrading. Any man who starts in life with that idea degenerates himself. He will never rise higher; he will never catch this glimpse from behind, he will always be a slave to the senses. He will struggle for the dollar that will get him a few cakes to eat. Better die than lead that life.*

Slowly, steadily, Vivekananda forced the subconscious to accept that getting your daily bread was not an end in itself, even though it may be a necessity.

But he was gentle. He did not expect anyone to acquire wisdom overnight. All he expected of you was that you realize where you stood.

- *Man makes a great mistake when he thinks that he can at once jump to the highest state. If a baby thinks he is going to be an old man in a day, he is mistaken…*
- *So, says the Vedanta, religion is to be realized now. And for you to become religious means that you will start without any religion, work your way up and realize things, see things for yourself; and when you have done that, then, and then alone, you have religion. Before that you are no better than atheists, or worse, because the atheist is sincere; he stands up and says, 'I do not know about these things,' while those others do not know but go about the world saying, 'We are very religious people.'*

My takeaway from Vivekananda, essentially, has been this – till the point I know nothing about the *reality* of religion or God, and what I 'know' is simply belief, custom, or hand-me-down thoughts from experts who also, in reality, know little of God, it is better to be clear and say, I do not know about these things. There is no point living for decades telling ourselves that 'we are very religious people' if we have not realized anything *directly*, for ourselves. Only by accepting that we start, essentially, without any religion, will we make the effort to work our way up.

> I am a spirit living in a body. I am not the body. The body will die, but I shall not die. Here am I in this body; it will fall, but I will go on living.
>
> – Vivekananda

Lesson 2: Food, clothes, books, rituals and places of worship are support systems to spirituality. But they are not religion.

> *Reason, theories, documents, doctrines, books, religious ceremonies are all helps to religion – religion itself consists in realization. We all say, there is a God. Have you seen God? That is the question… People have been fighting for ages, and what is the outcome? Intellect cannot reach there at all. We have to go beyond the intellect; the proof of religion is direct perception.*

The questions of what to eat, what to wear, what hand to use – it may have its rationality, but it is part of the outer support system. It is not religion. Following it does not mean you have understood anything of religion. Not following it does not damn you to hell. It is better to make mistakes trying to find your own answers, than to blindly allow someone else to tell you what faith is, and what God wants. God hasn't sub-contracted his work to the clergy of any faith.

> Vivekananda gave me the belief that questioning and searching was a truer form of following religion than falling at the feet of anyone dressed in saffron, white or black.

What did I learn from him? Essentially, all the things that irked me, made me awkward, sometimes even angry, things that I assumed were part of being religious – I could disengage from them, from ritualism, and from the collective participation in any sort of religious activity, and *still* follow what I was curious about.

Vivekananda gave me the belief that questioning and searching was a truer form of following religion than falling at the feet of anyone dressed in saffron, white or black.

At about eight years of age, I still remember registering that a particular *aarti* ended with a request to the deity to fill the home with wealth and prosperity, and take away all afflictions of the body. I vaguely recall having turned around and asked: How did people in the 'foreign' countries seemingly earn so much more money than we did, despite, I assume, not praying this way? I did not get a response, but what I did get was a reprimand for being insulting, and a quick request to the deity to forgive my impertinence, since I was but a foolish child.

I was confused for a while whether I had actually offended the deity and if that meant that I would have to lead a largely poor life as punishment. I tried to ask fewer questions for some time.

At 14, I put a few questions to a swami-ji who had been explaining that God would keep us safe and healthy as He cared for us. I asked him why God withdrew that affection when we become old. Why did he not keep us healthy then, and why could we not pray to Him for a lifespan of 150 years? And if we could not, and if the body did *not* matter, as it was transitional and meant to be just an instrument, and so on, then why was it worth asking Him to take care of it in the interim period? Why was there an expiry period for that caring?

Again, I did not get a response, but a pat on the head and the advice that 'in due course of time, you will understand these things'.

For someone carrying around such random questions, which went mostly unanswered, I then began to worry if having such questions in the mind amounted to some sort of sinful anti-God reflex?

Shortly thereafter, I picked up Vivekananda, and stumbled upon these lines:

> *He who wants to enter the realms of light must first give up this buying and selling, this 'shopkeeping' religion, and then enter the gates. It is not that you do not get what you pray for; you get everything, but such praying is a beggar's religion… 'A fool indeed is the man who, coming to a mine of diamonds, seeks for glass beads.' This body will die some time, so what is the use of praying for its health again and again? The wealthiest man can use and enjoy only a little portion of his wealth. We can never get all the things of this world, and if not, who cares?*

Reading this was a great relief. Finally, I had someone with the credentials to speak on these things, saying it was okay to be uncomfortable with such parts of religion.

Of course, it is not that I did not ever engage in 'shopkeeping'. I certainly did, and still do, but I'm aware that when I am praying for 'health and wealth', those are my weaker moments, not my finest.

During my teens and the twenties, this recurrent mental battle on the protocol of praying started – and has still not died.

If I have a sense of respect for someone or something or some place, I will be fine with wearing a dozen threads, fasting every other day, chanting a mantra, or doing anything else that may be seen to be a part of either my faith or traditions.

But I am uncomfortable doing all of this just because I have been *told* that it will supposedly bring me religious merit, material growth, better health, better appraisals and more… I will not carry a *tabeej* in my pocket for important meetings. I will not throw out all shirts of a specific colour because it is inauspicious. I will not recite any scripture as a chore, a task. If the *only* reason I am expected to do something is because a learned priest asks me, I tell myself to ignore it and let it be. Maybe, someday, *I'll* become a more learned priest and figure it out for myself.

So while the obsession with rituals irked Vivekananda – I liked it! The sharp, acidic tone of the monk derided fixation with formal worship, saying 'lying complacently on the bed and ringing the bell now and then is a sort of disease, pure and simple.' And then this was really, really hard:

- *Those whose heads have a tendency to be troubled day and night over such questions as whether the bell should ring on the right or on the left, whether the sandal-paste mark should be put on the head or somewhere else, whether the light should be waved twice or four times – simply deserve the name of wretches, and it is owing to that sort of notion that we are outcasts of Fortune…*
- *That such and such a chapter of such a Tantra has prescribed a standard length for the handle of a bell – what matters it to me? Through the Lord's will, out of your lips shall come millions of Vedas and Tantras and Puranas.*

Bit by bit, Vivekananda freed the mind from the needless baggage it had gathered.

However, it was not as if Vivekananda tore into every social custom or ritual simply as reflex. When he wrote on the practices pertaining to widow remarriage in India in that period, after explaining in some detail why some things were as they were, he added:

> *If it be necessary to change any social custom, the necessity underlying it should be found out first of all, and by altering it, the custom will die of itself. Otherwise no good will be done by condemnation or praise.*

This, track, too, was a recurrent one. When he felt a practice or a custom had a rationality to it that had perhaps been lost or forgotten over time, he asked critics to understand why it had begun and survived, before trashing it as regressive.

The other thing Vivekananda got into my otherwise conservative mind was an unlearning of the social protocol, a lessening of the nose-in-the-air approach at what 'these people' do. I am a teetotaller, a non-smoker and a vegetarian – by personal choice and not out of any sense of religious or social morality – and while I have my personal, philosophical take on animal life, it was illuminating for me to understand Vivekananda's responses on the topic of non-vegetarianism:

> *The taking of life is undoubtedly sinful; but so long as vegetable food is not made suitable to the human system through progress in chemistry, there is no other alternative but meat-eating. So long as*

man shall have to live a Râjasika (active) life under circumstances like the present, there is no other way except through meat-eating. It is true that the Emperor Asoka saved the lives of millions of animals by the threat of the sword; but is not the slavery of a thousand years more dreadful than that?

Beyond the larger, social perspective, he actively argued against equating the mere absence of eating meat with religious purity or superiority:

- *The cow does not eat meat, nor does the sheep. Are they great yogis? Any fool may abstain from eating this or that; surely that gives him no more distinction than to herbivorous animals. The man who will mercilessly cheat widows and orphans, and do the vilest deeds for money, is worse than any brute, even if he lives entirely on grass alone.*
- *The man whose heart never cherishes even the thought of injury to anyone, who rejoices at the prosperity of even his greatest enemy, that man is the Bhakta, he is the Yogi, he is the Guru of all, even though he lives every day of his life on the flesh of swine. Therefore we must always remember that external practices have value only as helps to develop internal purity. It is better to have internal purity alone, when minute attention to external observances is not practicable. But woe unto the man and woe unto the nation, that forgets the real, internal, spiritual essentials of religion, and mechanically clutches with death-grasp at all external forms and never lets them go.*

'External practices have value *only* as helps to develop internal purity.'

This was the stand he took, no matter what the external practice was.

What I found refreshing was the absence of the orthodox mind – of the list of pious and unholy traits that most preachers of religion seem to carry around in their pocket, to pull out and thrust in your face with the alacrity of a football linesman raising the flag for offside. Vivekananda's religiousness was not bound in by a closed orthodoxy. His approach to non-vegetarianism despite being a monk reminded me of Lincoln's approach to alcohol despite being a teetotaller – when rival generals complained to him about General Grant's excessive drinking habits, he famously suggested that they find out what brand of whisky he was having so Lincoln could send it to the other (victory-starved) generals in the hope that it may rub off on them.

In general, Vivekananda was wary of categorizing anything as impure, any action as sin, and was often critical of extreme passivity being mistaken for restraint. He was often irked by the 'rule book' or the 'commandments' model of being religious.

> *If living by rule alone ensures excellence, if it be virtue strictly to follow the rules and customs handed down through generations, say then, who is more virtuous than a tree, who is a greater devotee, a holier saint, than a railway train? Who has ever seen a piece of stone transgress a natural law? Who has ever known cattle to commit sin?*

He forced you to think for yourself, to question all basics – social as well as individual.

You may have read about the episode involving Vivekananda and the courtesan at the court of the maharaja of Khetri. In the context of the monk rarely taking a morally superior position, it is intriguing and educative.

The gist of the episode is as follows:

The maharaja of Khetri had invited Vivekananda to attend a performance in his company. Upon casual enquiry, the monk came to understand that the performance was to be a song by a courtesan. Morality outraged, the miffed monk – clearly expecting an evening of debauchery or its equivalent – thought it inappropriate for him to be present, and decided to get up and leave. The courtesan supposedly sent a request to him to stay on, which he, surprisingly enough, agreed to.

She, then, proceeded with the performance, which was, to Vivekananda's surprise and embarrassment, her singing Surdas' '*Prabhuji morey avagun chit na dharo*'. The suitably chastised Swami is said to have wept and then apologized to the girl for having prejudged her on account of her trade.

Some accounts portray the sequence differently, for instance, saying that he had refused to turn up in the first place, but came once he heard what she was singing. Which version has greater accuracy is inconsequential. The lesson here was that even a man as evolved as Vivekananda could fall prey to the ego of the saint, to the arrogance of moral superiority by which so many of us 'good people' are afflicted. But then, it was only a man as evolved as him who could recognize his error and not shy away from acknowledging it in public.

Each time I'm inclined to pass a sweeping judgment about someone because of their 'lifestyle', I try to remember the lesson he learnt. I still fail to apply it, often, but at least at the back of my mind, I know I've failed. We are often not as qualified to judge on grounds of morality as we like to think we are.

The Khetri episode took place when Vivekananda was 30. And then there was something which he wrote at 33, which I read in my early twenties and passed over at that point, not making too much sense of it. I read it again in my thirties – and this time I understood it a little better. Vivekananda himself wasn't reluctant to explain and accept how his emotional bandwidth expanded with exposure and learning over time:

> *At twenty years of age I was the most unsympathetic, uncompromising fanatic; I would not walk on the footpath on the theatre side of the streets in Calcutta. At thirty-three, I can live in the same house with prostitutes and never would think of saying a word of reproach to them. Is it degenerate? Or is it that I am broadening out into the Universal Love which is the Lord Himself? Again, I have heard that if one does not see the evil around him, he cannot do good work – he lapses into a sort of fatalism. I do not see that. On the other hand, my power of work is immensely increasing and becoming immensely effective. Some days, I get into a sort of ecstasy. I feel that I must bless every one, everything, love and embrace everything, and I do see that evil is a delusion.*

If Vivekananda doesn't have a perspective that comes from a high moral ground, where do we stand to have such a tone? Who are we to reproach people with the general vocabulary of the 'respectable' class – loose, fast, shallow, whatever?

An ordained monk, a man who says that he spoke to God himself in the form of Ramakrishna, writing that he was wrong in keeping a judgemental distance from 'those sort' of people, unapologetically saying that he could no longer see evil in their domain, that he can happily share a house with prostitutes. And this was in 1896.

If Vivekananda doesn't have a perspective that comes from a high moral ground, where do we stand to have such a tone?

Who are *we* to reproach people with the general vocabulary of the 'respectable' class – loose, fast, shallow, whatever? Each person will work out his or her own deal with the Universe. We can avoid doing what they do if it doesn't make sense to us, we can keep our distance if we are uncomfortable – but even then, we can't think of ourselves as morally superior and 'them' as morally inferior.

We simply don't know enough to do that.

Lesson 3: Criticize no one, for all doctrines and creeds have some good in them

> *Religious quarrels are always over the husks. When purity, when spirituality goes, leaving the soul dry, quarrels begin, and not before.*

Vivekananda embedded very firmly within me the thought that believing my religion – or what version of it I practise – was superior to any other could be arrogance, even stupidity. My pride in the religion that I was born into or acquired didn't give me the right to have contempt for what another had chosen to believe.

When, at different points of time, this view was contradicted, usually by people who supposedly had greater knowledge or pride, I did my best to gauge if *their* understanding of religion, and their practise of Hinduism, and their intensity of worshipping the Mother Goddess was superior to that of Ramakrishna and Vivekananda's. Despite my openness about their beliefs, none of them measured up to the benchmark of Vivekananda's thinking on religion. And so I ignored them and adhered to what the Swami had taught.

Don't be conceited about your beliefs; respect all, judge none. Don't care for sects and theories beyond a point:

- Vivekananda embedded very firmly within me the thought that believing my religion was superior to any other could be arrogance, even stupidity. My pride in the religion that I was born into or acquired didn't give me the right to have contempt for what another had chosen to believe.
- What I learnt from Vivekananda is to be devoid of conceit or a sense of superiority vis-à-vis any faith, sect or belief that is at divergence from what I was born into.
- Vivekananda never tired of reiterating Ramakrishna's teachings on the unity of all faiths. Given how frequently the world around us struggles to get the point, perhaps it is a teaching that needs incessant reiteration.
- If Ramakrishna and Vivekananda did not deem it fit to judge the faith of another after being as 'Hindu' and as evolved in matters of faith as they were, who am I, and what have I attained, to stand on any pedestal that declares any form of faith to be superior or inferior to another?
- Vivekananda bullies, badgers and begs us to be larger versions of ourselves, and not to confuse habit for goodness and sneering for superiority.
- This quote by Vivekananda talking of his master, sums it all: This is the message of Shri Ramakrishna to the modern world: 'Do not care for doctrines, do not care for dogmas, or sects, or churches, or temples; they count for little compared with the essence of existence in each man, which is spirituality; and the more this is developed in a man, the more powerful he is for good. Earn that first, acquire that, and criticize no one, for all doctrines and creeds have some good in them.'

What I learnt from Vivekananda is to be devoid of conceit or a sense of superiority vis-à-vis any faith, sect or belief that is at divergence from what I practice. Over the past few years, the sharpness of discourse on religion in India and in the world at large has been unsettling. Many of us seem to be fighting – often unsuccessfully – to establish that our place of birth, the religion our parents raised us in, the colour of our skin, the language we grew up speaking from the day we were born, and so on, give us a higher intellectual, social, or spiritual status than 'others'.

I have observed the paradox of 'religious' people frothing at the mouth, pumping their fists, and defending their religion, beliefs and culture at the top of their voices by usually trashing another belief or religion, irrespective of which faith they purportedly represent. Anger and sharpness radiate from them almost like a physical wave, and this has always reminded me of Vivekananda's warning:

Every vicious thought will rebound, every thought of hatred which you may have thought, in a cave even, is stored up, and will one day come back to you with tremendous power in the form of some misery here. If you project hatred and jealousy, they will rebound on you with compound interest. No power can avert them; when once you have put them in motion, you will have to bear them.

'Every vicious thought will rebound.'

Vivekananda reminds us that projecting hatred – on anything or anyone – will rebound on us, the haters. He reminds us that we cannot possibly associate hatred with religion. At least not the religion that he and Ramakrishna have spoken about.

Vivekananda never tired of reiterating Ramakrishna's teachings on the unity of all faiths. Given how frequently the world around us struggles to get the point, perhaps it is a teaching that *needs* constant reiteration. As we have seen earlier in the book, over a 100 years ago, Vivekananda quoted Ramakrishna to make this point:

> *My master used to say that these names as Hindu, Christian, etc., stand as great bars to all brotherly feelings between man and man. We must try to break them down first. They have lost all their good power and now stand as baneful influences under whose black magic even the best of us behave like demons.*

Vivekananda did not travel to distant lands to convert people to believe in his master or his faith. He did not tell them that the faith he was born into and then taught in a very practical manner was superior to any other. Instead of asking that his master be worshipped ahead of other masters, this was what he went around explaining:

> *This is the message of Shri Ramakrishna to the modern world: 'Do not care for doctrines, do not care for dogmas, or sects, or churches, or temples; they count for little compared with the essence of existence in each man, which is spirituality; and the more this is developed in a man, the more powerful he is for good. Earn that first, acquire that, and criticize no one, for all doctrines and creeds have some good in them.'*

Maybe we need to read these words once again, slower:

'Do not care for dogmas, or sects, or churches, or temples …'

Maybe we need to ask ourselves if we have moved away from Ramakrishna's understanding of religion – 'the essence of existence in each man, which is spirituality' – and have instead fixated on dogmas, temples, churches and sects.

It is a fair guess that Ramakrishna understood spirituality better than most religious advocates today, so before we worship their fiery loud beliefs, we should perhaps hear and reflect on what the calm man from Dakshineswar thought about all this.

If Ramakrishna and Vivekananda did not deem it fit to judge the faith of another after being as 'Hindu' and as evolved in matters of faith as they were, who am I, and what have I attained, to stand on any pedestal that declares any form of faith to be superior or inferior to another? What have any of us done that exceeds what they realized? They largely disengaged faith from political discourse, a lesson that is often lost in transmission, especially when it comes to Vivekananda.

What is our learning from his teachings? To begin with, we can perhaps do a reality check of all the traits, beliefs, mannerisms, rituals, dietary or cultural reflexes that are within us – did we choose them because we believed them to be the ideal, or because we have never known any other? Is it not possible that another individual who grew up speaking another tongue, having other meals, worshipping in another manner, absorbed all of that as ideal, just as we did? And is it not possible that *both* of us are right where we stand? Equally, if some appear to us as saints and some as sinners, are we really qualified to understand what they really are, or do we salute or sneer by habit? Can we be gentler and not rush to judge another who does not seem to share our habits or our morality?

Ramakrishna's disciple, the morally upright saint, paradoxically, teaches us to not overrate sainthood or morality – at least not in the way we are socially conditioned to define it.

What is our takeaway from the vision of Vivekananda in a world that is increasingly polarized along ideology and faith?

If we infer that anyone who dons religious robes is true and virtuous and is the custodian of thousands of years of evolved spirituality, we are being naïve. If, on the other hand, we run down all that tradition and history have passed on to us, find a misplaced sense of superiority in dismissing everything associated with India's roots, we are being needlessly cynical, perhaps even disrespectful.

The answer, perhaps, is somewhere along the Buddha's Middle Path, or Aristotle's Golden Mean. The answer is in realizing that the strength of the philosophy that Ramakrishna and Vivekananda practised and preached lies in its largeness of heart and intellect. If we genuinely study and understand them, the fundamental contradiction in angrily defending them, or the faith or the nation they were born into, will become clear to us.

Vivekananda's faith did not need him to run down other faiths. He had learnt from the example of Ramakrishna, who worshipped intensely, even madly, at the temple of Kali, but never had a word to say against a church or a mosque. His religious experiences – he had moved beyond mere beliefs – left no scope for pettiness within.

Vivekananda's love for his motherland did not instill in him a hatred for other lands, not even the land that ruled India politically throughout his lifetime. He was so secure in his beliefs and so intense in his affections that he never needed to validate them through the trashing of the beliefs and affections of others. He did not need to respect the priesthood to prove his faith in God. He loved his motherland intensely, understood both its strengths and weaknesses, and so did not feel the need to give speeches trashing Englishmen; he instead applied his efforts in telling his fellow men what would give them strength. An intensely self-assured man, he did not let his pride harden him into someone who could not think beyond his country, his faith, and his master.

> Vivekananda was a gentle giant, and even when we are dazzled by the magnitude of his intellect, we must not forget the gentleness of his spirit.

If we think we admire or follow Vivekananda, and if we, at the same time, find ourselves increasingly angry, unforgiving, or dismissive of those whose ideologies are dissimilar to ours, perhaps we should take a little time to pause and introspect. In his own manner, Vivekananda was a gentle giant, and even when we are dazzled by the magnitude of his intellect, we must not forget the gentleness of his spirit.

> *Religion must be studied on a broader basis than formerly. All narrow, limited, fighting ideas of religion have to go. All sect ideas and tribal or national ideas of religion must be given up. That each tribe or nation should have its own particular God, and think that every other is wrong, is a superstition and should belong to the past. All such ideas must be abandoned.*

The man who said this would say the same for all manners of thought, not just religion – that all narrow, limited, fighting ideas must go. That we must widen and expand our understanding, our intellect and our compassion, not lock ourselves into forts and assume we are besieged. Vivekananda bullies, badgers and begs us to be larger versions of ourselves, and not to confuse habit for goodness and sneering for superiority.

And then he reminds us, yet again:

> *The second idea that I learnt from my Master, and which is perhaps the most vital, is the wonderful truth that the religions of the world are not contradictory or antagonistic. They are but various phases of one eternal religion. That one eternal religion is applied to different planes of existence, is applied to the opinions of various minds and various races. There never was my religion or yours, my national religion or your national religion; there never existed many religions, there is only the one. One infinite religion existed all through eternity and will ever exist, and this religion is expressing itself in various countries in*

various ways. Therefore we must respect all religions and we must try to accept them all as far as we can.

Vivekananda learnt many lessons from Ramakrishna that reflect this sentiment, lessons that repeatedly emphasize the basic concept of religious coexistence, the absence of conflict, the futility of seeking superiority. And this thought is repeated, clearly and vividly, till the point that there can be no doubt whatsoever as to what Ramakrishna thought about conflict between religions. I would like to leave a few of Vivekananda's words with you for you to draw your own interpretations:

I am a disciple of Ramakrishna Paramahamsa, a perfect Sannyasin whose influence and ideas I fell under. This great Sannyasin never assumed the negative or critical attitude towards other religions, but showed their positive side how they could be carried into life and practised. To fight, to assume the antagonistic attitude, is the exact contrary of his teaching, which dwells on the truth that the world is moved by love.

'To fight, to assume the antagonistic attitude, is the exact contrary of his teachings.'

The exact contrary.

Ramakrishna himself would use the simplest of language to explain to his followers what he thought:

There are several bathing ghats in a large tank. Whoever goes to whichever ghat he pleases to take a bath, or to fill his vessel, reaches the water, and it is useless to quarrel with one another claiming one's ghat to be better than another's... Every religion of the world is one ghat. Go direct with a sincere and earnest heart through any one of these ghats, and you shall reach the water of Eternal Bliss. But say not that your religion is better that of another.

'Say not that your religion is better than that of another.'

The above words make it clear that he spoke from actual practice, not generic goodwill. How many of us remember or are aware of this part of Ramakrishna's journey, which was the basis for his belief in the essential unity of faiths? Hear it in Vivekananda's words:

> *The next desire that seized upon the soul of this man was to know the truth about the various religions. Up to that time, he had not known any religion but his own. He wanted to understand what other religions were like. So he sought teachers of other religions. He found a Mahommedan Saint and went to live with him; he underwent the disciplines prescribed by him, and to his astonishment found that when faithfully carried out, these devotional methods led him to the same goal he had already attained. He gathered similar experience from following the true religion of Jesus the Christ.*
>
> *He went to all the sects he could find, and whatever he took up, he went into it with his whole heart. He did exactly as he was told, and in every instance, he arrived at the same result. Thus, from actual experience he came to know that the goal of every religion is the same, that each is trying to teach the same thing, the difference being largely in method, and still more in language.*

This is not abstract philosophy. This is the hunger, beyond what we will ever have, to understand things in the realm of faith. And since Ramakrishna says these words after having searched for the truth this way, it is right to accept that he knew what he was talking about more than any of the present-day gurus we follow for guidance.

But if you step out in the world, there are a thousand 'experts' on religion and ten thousand 'defenders' of faiths, all telling you, very loudly, what is right and what is wrong, who is a 'true' believer of a faith and who is not, issuing certificates of whether or not you are a good

Hindu, a devout Muslim or a Christian abiding by the Lord's teachings.

I have never figured out how – and why – I should accept that they understand what God expects of me better than I understand myself. Has God spoken to them like he did to Ramakrishna? If not, why is their word weightier than mine? Because they spend more time in temples, mosques and churches, and dress a certain way? I don't think I can buy that – not after reading Ramakrishna and Vivekananda. The bar to being a guru is much higher once you have encountered the minds and hearts of these two.

There is a question from Vivekananda, brief in structure and simple in tone, that resonates with me in this context. It is a question that perhaps needs to be raised more often, across the globe, in all countries, to the upholders and guardians of *all* faiths, and to their cheering followers:

> *I do not understand how people declare themselves to be believers in God, and at the same time think that God has handed over to a little body of men all truth, and they are the guardians of the rest of humanity.*

I do not understand either. Do you?

Who exactly hands over the filter of truth to some, for them to declare to the rest of us what it is? Have they found the truth for themselves? How do they judge me any better than I can judge them?

I do not want intermediaries between myself and the powers above. Heaven, hell or nowhere, I will find my way myself, thank you.

Lesson 4: Be comfortable with not knowing, and learn to trust the unknown. Don't play God.

After telling you to do your best, to not live through your years on the planet passively, Vivekananda also reminds you – more in the form of lessons you infer from his life than from his formal teachings – that there are things beyond our control and comprehension. That we are not essential for the world to go on. That sometimes by instinct and by reflex the 'I' becomes grand and we think that we can support, patronize, assist and help others.

This is a lie.

We can try, but what we do is for *our* growth, our learning. Nobody depends upon our help.

Towards his later years, in particular, having done his duty across the world, Vivekananda would come back to such thoughts more frequently.

> *Whatever has happened is now past – it is all the result of past Karma. What is the good of my repentance? I do not believe it. It is all Karma. Whatever of Mother's work has to be accomplished through me, She made me do, and has now flung me aside, breaking down my body and mind. Her will be done!*

At another point, advising an associate on the sense of duty towards others, he explains:

> *Things go on all right whether we lend them our helping hands or not. We in delusion only break ourselves. There is a false sentiment which goes to the extreme of unselfishness, only to injure others by its submission to every evil.*

I took some years to absorb the first quote here. Our sense of ego and self-importance makes us believe that our presence is vital to all that we are part of. It may well be true, but it is equally true that the capacity of systems to adapt to our absence is also fairly high. One of the simplest tests we face is when we are knocked out of action unexpectedly – from our college, office, or cricket team – by, say, an injury that will take a few weeks to heal. In most instances, no matter how essential we were while we were fit and functional, things get handled almost as well in our unexpected absence. How often do you see this in sports: a key player suffers an injury mid-tournament and a collective wail goes up amongst fans – only for the replacement to soon be hailed as the new shining star!

It is a good idea to take ourselves less seriously. The world did fine before we were born, and it will manage just as well after we die – let us work, yes, but let us not self-assign delusionally grand roles to ourselves.

As bosses, parents, 'seniors' and elders, we often tend to overrate our importance, over-protect people and systems, and, as Vivekananda says, sometimes, in delusion of our absolute indispensability, break ourselves. On the other hand, the doting, excessively protective parent who overlooks everything a child does out of 'love', and says, 'after all, everything is for our children', personifies the false sentiment that only ends up injuring others – including those it is supposedly protecting – by submitting to everything.

It is a good idea, therefore, to take ourselves less seriously. The world did fine before we were born, and it will manage just as well after we die – let us work, yes, but let us not self-assign delusionally grand roles to ourselves.

Not very long before the final year of his life, he wrote:

Moths like me die by the thousand every instant. Her work goes on all the same… Alone and drifting about in the will-current of the Mother has been my whole life… I am free. I am Mother's child. She works, she plays. Why should I plan? What should I plan? Things came and went, just as She liked, without my planning. We are Her automata. She is the wirepuller.

The most memorable lesson on this, for me, was – for want of a better description – the reprimand Vivekananda received at Kheer Bhawani.

This temple has a special place in the reference points of my life, for the basic thought that I picked up from the lesson Vivekananda learnt here is a mind-altering one. I read this portion about Vivekananda's journey to Amarnath and Kheer Bhawani in *Talks With Swami Vivekananda* and it has stayed with me since:

> A few days after returning to Srinagar, he went to visit Kshir Bhavani Devi and staying there for seven days worshipped the Devi and made Homa to her with offerings of Kshira (condensed milk). Every day, he used to worship the Devi with a *maund* of Kshira as offering. One day, while worshipping, the thought arose in Swamiji's mind: 'Mother Bhavani has been manifesting Her Presence here for untold years. The Mohammedans came and destroyed her temple, yet the people of the place did nothing to protect Her. Alas, if I were then living I could never have borne it silently.'
>
> When, thinking thus, his mind much oppressed with sorrow and anguish, he distinctly heard the voice of the Mother: 'It was according to My desire that the Mohammedans destroyed this temple. *It is My desire that I should live in a*

> *dilapidated temple, otherwise, can I not immediately erect a seven-storeyed temple of gold here if I like? What can you do? Shall I protect you or shall you protect me!*'
>
> Swamiji said, 'Since hearing that divine voice, I cherish no more plans. The idea of building *maths* etc. I have given up; as Mother wills, so it will be.' The disciple, speechless with wonder, began to think, 'Did he not one day tell me that whatever I saw and heard was but the echo of the Atman within me, that there was nothing outside?' – and fearlessly spoke it out also – 'Sir, you used to say that Divine Voices are the echo of our inward thoughts and feelings.' Swamiji gravely said, 'Whether it be internal or external, if you actually hear with your ears such a disembodied voice, as I have done, can you deny it and call it false? Divine Voices are actually heard, just as you and I are talking.'

This was the most surreal, most fun-filled, and most educative conversation between God and man that I had ever heard.

'Do you think I cannot erect a seven-storey temple of gold here *if I want to*? Shall *I* protect *you*, or will *you* protect *me*?'

I laughed when I read this, decades back, and I still can't resist a smile each time I think about it. That question addressed to Vivekananda – whether we believe it happened physically or in an alternate mindspace is irrelevant – is almost surreal in the world that we live in now where temples, mosques and churches tend to be perceived as things man has to fight for in order to deliver God His due.

We are all fighting to protect our God. All religions are under attack, all faiths are embattled. All believers are willing to take up the sword – or at least social media – across the planet to protect Him, by whatever name they call Him. Or Her.

But will She protect us, or will we protect Her? Will we defend God? Will we protect religion? As if God needs us overzealous inhabitants of this microscopic planet to rise to His defence! The naivety of it all. What would Vivekananda have made of it today?

A new convert to Vivekananda's philosophy at that point, I had just about finished college, and had begun to look with curiosity and admiration at him as a man who never took a false step. When I read this, it made me think for many days, and see him and my recently formed views in a new light. I have never since then overrated my relevance as the defender of anything in the philosophical or religious space.

Does God need protection?
Will we defend Him? Seriously?

We are all fighting to protect our God. All religions are under attack, all faiths are embattled. All believers are willing to take up the sword – or at least social media – across the planet to protect Him, by whatever name they call Him. Or Her.

But will She protect us, or will we protect Her? Will we defend God? Will we protect religion? As if God needs us overzealous inhabitants of this microscopic planet to rise to His defence! The naivety of it all. What would Vivekananda have made of it today?

We grow up making deals with Him/Her and submit offerings at temples. Sometimes, we even bizarrely describe them as 'donations'. But what do we possibly have to offer that the Creator of the Universe needs? What we offer or donate is for our internal peace, for a sense of fulfilment, for exercise in our own 'moral gymnasium', as Vivekananda says. It would help us to remember that She can erect a 'seven-storey temple of gold' anywhere, anytime, if She wants to – but She does not *need* our help. What little we ever do is a gesture of our affection. We will all be gone soon and everything will go on, the way She wants it to. By whatever name we call Her. For, lest we limit Vivekananda's vision, let us remember, as Sister Nivedita recollected, he offered flowers at the feet of the Virgin Mary in a chapel in Switzerland in the summer of 1896 and, turning to Nivedita, explained, 'For she is also the Mother.'

Postscript:

A year or so after first reading this part, I made up my mind to visit the temple. I was in any case living in Jammu and Kashmir during the years I first picked up and absorbed Vivekananda. As my father was part of the state's administrative machinery, we spent some time in both Srinagar and Jammu.

During one of my visits from Jammu to Srinagar, I began to make plans to reach the shrine. It is, after all, less than an hour's drive out of the city. Here, however, there was a catch. The assignment that my father then occupied in the state's administration meant that travelling that distance was not so simple. It was the 1990s and militancy was on the upswing in Kashmir. Downtown Srinagar and the highways around the city were not places senior functionaries or people related to them ventured into casually. Threats of abduction, or worse, of people related to those in the state security machinery were not uncommon. In Srinagar, all I was allowed was a stroll within a 500-yard radius of the front gate of the house in a 'high security zone'.

The drive to Kheer Bhawani was to be taken up on a day when adequate security was available. For a variety of reasons, it was not working out. Security men weren't available. The escort vehicles deputed with my father would get free only by night, when driving on those roads was seen to be risky. I kept waiting for a week for that hour-long journey to materialize, pacing restlessly around the house, or on the stretch outside the gate.

After a week, a gentleman came over to meet my father over breakfast. I only knew him as Haji Sahab. From his headgear, immaculately maintained beard and demeanour, I assumed he was a cleric. A copy of the Quran, which he had brought back from the Haj, occupied pride of place in our study-plus-puja room. Once he had finished discussing his work in our drawing room, I made my way there. He gently turned to me and asked what I was doing in the city, and what all I had seen so far. I used the opportunity to promptly launch forth on my tale of grievances. The conversation went ahead for a couple of minutes. He then turned to my father and said, 'I'll take him. He will be completely safe.'

I have always believed that the sheer unexpectedness of it and the courtesy that was due to him as a guest saved that proposal from being shot down. An hour later, with no security or escort, but clad in a *pheran* and a fur cap, I drove out with Haji Sahab in his ageing Maruti 800. He took me through roads and by-lanes, where, he explained gently, the vehicles of security forces would usually enter only when escorted by a multi-vehicle cavalcade with mounted light machine guns. On the journey, he patiently heard my Vivekananda story.

Once we reached Kheer Bhawani, he waited two hours as I walked around and attempted to absorb the vibes of the place where the Mother Goddess had given Vivekananda a dressing down for forgetting who the Protector in the equation was. It was both deeply engaging and surreal. After I had had my philosophical fill of the place, he drove me back as I stayed quiet, mulling over the beautiful contradictions of that short journey.

It was only later, in hindsight, that it occurred to me that a Haji ended up taking me to the temple that Vivekananda was worked up about on account of it being destroyed by 'the Mohammedans' at some point in history. A Kashmiri cleric navigated an officer's son's visit to a temple through militancy-afflicted Srinagar.

Ironic? Poetic? Make of it what you will.

It seemed apt to reflect on what the Goddess had told Vivekananda a 100 years back at that very spot – will we take the decisions, or, as always, will She?

I said a silent word of gratitude to Vivekananda – for crossing the line of self-importance and inviting that reprimand, because the incident has so much to teach us.

And so, these four general lessons were my takeaways. There are, of course, thousands of words that can be written both on the subject and on the man. To simplify it, then, as to what is religion, and what is not, a simple rule of thumb may help.

Does it petrify? Does it scare? Does it intimidate? Then there is a good chance that it is a ritual, a tradition, even a practice or a custom – but it is not spiritual. If it weakens you or leaves you feeling inferior, smaller, scared, then whatever *else* it is, it is not religion. Trust Vivekananda on this. Absolutely.

> *The best guide in life is strength. In religion, as in all other matters, discard everything that weakens you, have nothing to do with it.*

Summing up, this is how Vivekananda helped me deal with myself:

- I learnt that solitude is fine, that dependence on others should be minimal, and that doubt is not weakness, but essential for growth. He kept me immune from the pressures of popularity and people-pleasing. 'I do not care who comes or who goes,' he declared.

- I was able to tame my baser instincts of getting into a fight, whether on the road or online. He reminded me that silence is a legitimate answer to flak when it comes from habitual detractors and fault-finders.
- He reminded me that we are prone to excessive caution, excessive care, excessive fear – but is life really 'such a sweet thing' for us to obsess with safeguarding it, 24/7?
- We are wired to hold on to some things hard, but he thinks differently. At least, he forced me to pause once in a while to remember what he said: 'Let name and fame and money go, they are a terrible bondage!'
- The very reflex of trying too hard to hold on to things, trying too hard to not get things wrong, can often achieve just the opposite: 'He who is afraid of loss, always loses!' He trained me to soften my grip and not let 'loss' be so shattering.
- He demonstrated that death can be approached, philosophically, as a natural stage, without panic or fear, almost with detachment. It may be a challenge, but through him at least I can see that it is possible.
- I learnt not to confuse rituals with religion – a frequent error that many people make.
- He encouraged me to question, sort my doubts, rather than fall blindly at the feet of those who declare they are knowledgeable in matters of faith.
- I learnt not to take the high moral ground merely on account of where I was born and the practices I inherited. He warned me that it is easy to think of conceit as 'pride'.

- No matter what religion I practice, he reminded me that I must do away with a sense of hierarchy. 'All narrow, limited, fighting ideas of religion have to go.'
- Finally, after extensively trimming my ego, he served, and continues to do so, a key reminder in the man-God relationship: Is our vanity confusing us about who protects whom? We are passing through here for a few decades; the Universe has been around for longer than we can count. Will we protect Her, or will She protect us? Don't take yourself so seriously so as to think that the Almighty needs your 'protection'.

Part 2

Dealing with Work

What Can a Monk Teach Us About Working in an Office?

Can Vivekananda be a reference point to handle work? This is a topic that I have been obsessively engaged with for a couple of decades. My colleagues have sometimes wondered whether a practitioner of an 'other-worldly' philosophy can have inputs relevant to the practical, everyday issues of the workplace. But in the span of my mid-level career, Vivekananda has been a very relevant guide, often offering more practical and sustainable suggestions than life coaches and HR experts.

He may have not been an entrepreneur or a teacher of management theory, but the fundamental truths he taught with such fire and passion have a surprisingly high degree of relevance in our workplaces – zones where our ambition, impatience and anger can sometimes make us resentful far quicker than is justified, more so when things don't go our way. He doesn't write a road map on how to find your way, but he can help you manage yourself when you don't have one.

Young people just starting out at work have to battle emotional, social and psychological challenges that the initial years bring. The older worker, on the other hand, if not enthroned on a plush swivel chair in a corner cabin, has to take care not to be caught in a cynical, self-defeating mindset. Vivekananda helps both the young and the old battle their demons.

I began my career at a very average salary in a very small organization with a very non-glamorous job. I was not from IIT, IIM, St. Stephen's or JNU, and so when I tell young people who pass out of blue-chip institutes and join nationally renowned brands that I envy them because my first job was so different from theirs – they think it's just an old person rambling in the 'Oh-our-life-was-so-much-harder-than-yours' tone.

It *was*, but that's not the point. The point is that across my 25 years in salaried jobs, I have faced the same questions, issues, dilemmas, happiness and heartbreak, conflicts, people battles, gratitude, thanklessness, anger, frustration and validation as most of us do as we chart out our professional lives. Almost without fail, Vivekananda has been there to calm my mind whenever I was unsure or felt unsettled.

> **Vivekananda, the problem-solver**
>
> I turned to Vivekananda when faced with questions about work, without really planning to, but they worked so well for my mental clarity that I felt little need to turn to management experts.

I approach many basic life questions from a Vivekananda-centric prism. Given that over half our life is spent at work anyway (even when we are in Work from Home mode for a bit, it's not as if work takes any less of our time and mindspace), many of his life lessons and work lessons tend to merge into each other over time.

I turned to Vivekananda when faced with questions about work, without really planning to, but they worked so well for my mental clarity that, thereafter, I felt little need to turn to management experts. While some of his answers worked for me perfectly, as they were, others I understood in my own context. As I processed them, I was then able to go beyond and find my own answers.

Some of them may work for you, too.

The basic clarity of his thought and the fundamental truths that he taught are surprisingly relevant to contemporary workplaces – that, more often than not, have difficult choices, conflicting views, long hours, just about adequate money, flak, gossip, alignments… you know the story. These, I categorize as the skirmishes of the work zone. Then, there is also the big battle of competing, addressing your own irrelevance and obsolescence, and staying ahead in the rat race.

Once in that race, ambition and impatience often get the better of us, keeping us edgy, envious, and even resentful of the relative success of others. Vivekananda softly points out the irrelevance of it all.

Starting a Career: The Initial Years and the Basics

WHAT DO I WANT to be?

Vivekananda changed a key basic very early in my life, just at the time I was starting out on my own. He redefined the question we all ask ourselves in our growing years: What do I want to be? This is a tough question to answer, especially when replies like 'I want to be a doctor' or 'I will go to IIT' are not part of the answer.

S Radhakrishan, in his commentary on the Gita, had already planted the seed of this thought in my head, as he explained II.53:

> *We must act, but with equanimity, which is more important than any action. The question is not* what *shall we do, but* how *shall we do it? In what spirit shall we act?*

And as the idea of the *how* shall we do it became the primary one, the need for a guide to have that conversation with became important. And there was Vivekananda – waiting to answer all those questions.

A few years back, I chanced upon this from *The Undoing Project* by Michael Lewis – a look at the contributions of two Israeli psychologists. One of them, Amos Tversky, made this point that I could relate to, and you'll figure out why:

'It's hard to know how people select a course in life. The big choices we make are practically random. The small choices probably tell us more about who we are. Which field we go into may depend on which high school teacher we happened to meet. Who we marry may depend on who happens to be around at the right time of life. On the other hand, the small decisions are very systematic. That I became a psychologist is probably not very revealing. *What kind* of psychologist I am may reflect deep traits.'

The inference is that while thinking about the *nature* of the work we will get into tends to take up 90 per cent of our focus, when we think about careers and jobs, perhaps we should be more conscious about what *kind* of workers we will be, irrespective of roles and professions.

'No work is petty'

My first full-time job was in a newly established newspaper in Jammu. It did not sell much. Working there did not bring with it any prestige and power, and hardly any money. I was still struggling to form a clear career plan and joining that newspaper at that point was a very unplanned call, taken more in an immediate personal context rather than as part of any structured plan. Therefore, it was just by reflex that *whatever* came my way in that tucked-away-in-a-by-lane office, I did as well as I could.

But it was in the back of beyond, and, almost as soon as I started working there, I feared I would be lost during my best years, reduced to an inconsequential and irrelevant entity. It was not a question of ego or visibility, but of not stagnating at the very outset of my career. Again, it was Vivekananda who came to my rescue as I nursed my injuries from emotional and intellectual skirmishes.

Stuck in what I saw as relatively low-profile tasks in a monotonous system, when I yearned for more challenging things and had thoughts of abruptly walking off, he advised me to not be an impulsive young idiot.

> *Even the greatest fool can accomplish a task if it be after his heart. But the intelligent man is he who can convert every work into one that suits his taste. No work is petty... He indeed is intelligent who notices this and succeeds in making all work truly great.*

'No work is petty':

I tried to not be 'the greatest fool' and to learn to make whatever work there was at hand into something worth doing better. And I learnt – for life – that no work is petty. It paid off, even if in the smallest of ways. It taught me to respect *all* work – the routine, the mechanical, the behind-the-scenes tasks, not just the theatrical and the flamboyant.

It is a key lesson for the initial years. We are frustrated easily because 'this' is not what we 'want to do'. If we have to do something we had not signed up for, we chafe, feel bound, hedged in, and as a result, do it badly and long to escape. Accommodating to any task is seen as drudgery, even soul-sapping.

Vivekananda gives us another perspective, one not very popular in today's world: The intelligent individual is he who can convert *every work* into one that suits his taste. It may not be possible, of course, for us to gel well with things that are complete misfits with our personalities, but we can still pay heed to him. We can at least try to remember that in due course, even the most exciting of roles can get monotonous, the romance can wear off and the reality seem less fascinating. A conscious effort to handle well even what we did *not* love at first sight may, therefore, in the long run, prove to be a valuable reflex to acquire.

Vivekananda's core lessons for the workplace:

- No work is petty.
- The intelligent man is he who can convert every work into one that suits his taste.
- By doing well the duty which is nearest to us...we make ourselves stronger.
- That man who does his duty as he goes, putting his shoulder to the wheel, higher and higher duties will fall to his share.

In short, what I learnt was: Do your duty as you go along, and do the work that is in your hands now, to the best of your ability. Make this your default setting at work.

In that seemingly insignificant office in a nondescript by-lane in Jammu, when my small role was made even smaller, and I was assigned the most inconsequential page in terms of content, my first reflex was to fret and fume. But then I went back to a) Radhakrishnan's '*how* shall we do it?' and b) Vivekananda's 'even the greatest fool...' and changed the way I looked at it.

Instead of finding sympathetic colleagues to unburden my angst, I worked to try and make it the most interesting page of the paper by learning the basics of layout and obstinately working twice the required hours. After a couple of months of being at it, day in and day out, the designer working on the front page looked at my handiwork for the day, nodded appreciatively, and remarked, 'If you keep doing things this way, one day, you will even make the front page of this paper!'

A few months later, I did make the front page of that paper. I continued with the same approach to whatever was assigned to me. And in less than 24 months, I became the editor. Long after I moved out of that organization, and later from that city, the fact that Vivekananda's lesson *actually worked*, stayed with me. Thereafter, I rarely made the mistake of assuming the work I was handling on any given day was beneath me. If it was not fascinating at the very outset, I at least tried to deliver my best in whatever situation I found myself in.

A couple of years later, in a much bigger organization, in a bigger city, I had a change of assignment. I had joined up for Department X, but was asked to move to Department Y, which was unfamiliar territory. I had no major disagreements, saw it as a challenge, and agreed. It was not seen as a very wise choice and the general sense was that I had agreed only because I was too junior to have refused. Colleagues sympathized with me, foreseeing me shortly fading into obscurity.

I took out a print of this viewpoint of Vivekananda's and tacked it up on my workstation – something that I had begun to pay attention to during my early battles at the workplace. By now, I had begun to have great faith in what he was telling me about work.

- *By doing well the duty which is nearest to us, the duty which is in our hands now, we make ourselves stronger... We find ourselves in the position for which we are fit, and if one has some capacity above another, the world will find it out too....*
- *He who grumbles at the little thing that has fallen to his lot to do, will grumble at everything. Always grumbling, he will lead a miserable life. But that man who does his duty as he goes, putting his shoulder to the wheel, higher and higher duties will fall to his share.*

This is a very important lesson to learn in terms of managing our own moods and expectations. As a natural reflex, we tend to often draw our sense of self-esteem and validation from the perceived importance or stature of the task that we have been entrusted with. If the task given to us is not considered valuable, we are irked, disinterested, or both. We, therefore, do it half-heartedly or cannot bring ourselves to put our best into it.

Does that help us achieve what we originally wanted to do? Hardly. In all likelihood, we are judged by our system as being incapable of even delivering the 'less complicated' tasks properly. That further reduces our likelihood of being able to have our own priorities taken seriously. We then get disillusioned and think that 'this place' is incapable of appreciating our true talents.

It is a spiral that leads nowhere and is more likely to leave us embittered and disgruntled than anything else.

Vivekananda is giving us some very clear emotional and behavioural guidelines here:

1. *Always* do, to the best of your ability, the 'duty nearest' to you. Is it just a ten-minute-long side role in a movie, and not that of the lead? Or a teaching role in a distant village school, and not a professorship at an IIM? Or, perhaps a sidelined, inconsequential beat in a small newspaper, and not the anchoring of a primetime TV show? Or a punitive transfer to a godforsaken government department, and not the prize posting you thought you deserved on merit? Had you joined up for one wing but got shifted to another, much to your dismay, as your organization realigned priorities in the COVID-19 meltdown?

   It's all right.

   Whatever the world places nearest to you, *do it well*. It is your way of working that is being tested, no matter what the work is. Don't lower your benchmarks to meet the average, irrelevant, and inconsequential task assigned to you. The *task* may carry that branding, but *you* do not have to, on that account, be an average, irrelevant and inconsequential worker. If you think that you have 'some capacity above another', it cannot be ignored for long. In fact, in a 'side job', given that most would have attempted it only half-heartedly, the scope to demonstrate that you can do something exceptional is far greater than in a prize assignment. It gives you greater opportunity to let the world find out what you can do, and how you do things in general.

2. Don't crib. Even though it often makes you feel better to have friends enthusiastically agree that everyone else is wrong and you have been dealt out great injustice, it doesn't help. Grumbling at the 'little thing that has fallen to your lot' and doing it while moaning all the while that you would rather not be doing it, is such a waste of your time, energy and talent. It is not an investment in a career. Such a worker, Vivekananda says, will 'grumble at everything' and lead a miserable life, and over time, this will become his or her second nature. Many years after reading this, I noticed a phrase in a very engaging book, *Rules and Tools for Leaders,* by a retired major general of the US Air Force, Perry M Smith, that seemed a perfect fit. Smith called certain types of workers the 'chronic malcontents'. Turning into a chronic malcontent is something we need to guard against. Fitting that template will of course let us have a loud, usually dismissive, opinion on everyone and everything, but it most probably won't lead to a career that one can look back at with a sense of satisfaction.

Let's check if we recurrently tend to grumble at the 'little things' that come our way. If we do, there's a fair chance that great things won't. This topic is unpleasant, but deal with it we must, and be self-critical if necessary.

3. 'Put your shoulder to the wheel' wherever you go. No matter how small, low-profile, or damaging to the ego

it is – if there is a task you have taken on, then put your shoulder to the wheel and *make* a difference. Else, don't take it on. Give the work the same respect you would if you were the police commissioner of New York or an admiral aboard an aircraft carrier in the Pacific. If you do that, over time, higher and higher duties *will* fall to your share. From Eisenhower's meteoric rise during WWII to Virat Kohli's rapid ascent to the captaincy of the Indian cricket team, there are a 1,00,000 examples to demonstrate that when someone does the *primary* task they are entrusted with, passionately and methodically, higher roles are frequently, even unexpectedly, thrust upon them, even if they weren't lobbying for the post.

When you don't have the top job, don't drift – slog even harder. We sometimes respond with tears when the situation demands sweat.

These Vivekananda core lessons enabled me to retain a sense of balance during my early years, the tempestuous twenties in particular. Over extended periods of time, I did not obsess over the lack of relevance, glamour, or importance of *what* my work on any given day was, but instead, whatever it happened to be, I focused on *how* to do it better.

Over a longer period, I have not had reason to change that reflex of the twenties. If anything, as you gain experience, you begin to understand that no matter what your role – start-up CEO, district police chief, movie director, newspaper editor, army officer, surgeon – you never, *ever* can be 100 per cent in control of what you are doing.

Your field transfer request can be turned down, your enterprise can be impacted by changing economic policies, your movie may be held up by the censor board or by angry vigilantes or by theatres being locked down on account of

COVID-19, your 'dream job' company may be struggling to just stay afloat as the aforementioned lockdown trips all growth plans. External situations, competitors, seniors and a dozen other factors can – and often will – derail your plans. That is how it is.

HR uses cryptic acronyms like VUCA these days to describe the work universe – Volatility, Uncertainty, Complexity and Ambiguity. These are more or less a given now. Instead of feeling overwhelmed or oppressed, we may as well learn how to deal with them.

Even when you control most of what you do, you can't control the results. Some great products, brilliant movies, and engaging books almost inexplicably fail, while some very ordinary ones rake in millions. Of course, brilliant and ordinary are subjective, but you probably know what I mean. The point is, seeking a sense of satisfaction entirely from a) what you are doing (nature of work), and b) how it rewards you (degree of material success), is a risky model, since work in the real world is not a chemistry lab reaction where adding A to B leads to C.

Seeking satisfaction instead, in *how* you do what you do, in putting your shoulder to the wheel, in doing 'well', the duty *nearest* to you – is an alternate route to a more peaceful and perhaps less angst-filled journey through the workplace. It may not be the default route, and it is definitely not the only route, but it *is* an alternative route worth considering.

Remember the basics. Do your duty as you go along, and do the work that is in your hands *now,* to the best of your ability. Better still, make it your default setting. And leave it at that. More often than not, the rest will follow of its own accord.

'When you are doing any work, do not think of anything beyond'

When you look to what is in your hands now, and to do it to the best of your ability, what exactly does that mean? What is the best of your ability? How do you attain it? There is another Vivekananda lesson here that helps.

> *When you are doing any work, do not think of anything beyond. Do it as worship, as the highest worship, and devote your whole life to it for the time being.*

He said this over a century ago. Today, perhaps more than at any point in human history, we struggle to have any space where we 'do not think of anything beyond'. There is so much to consume, so much competing for our mindspace. People struggle to write for a bit without checking their mail, seeing Twitter, checking WhatsApp, posting on Instagram and so on. We can't concentrate on any one thing for long. Even when we drive, the police have to threaten to lock us up, fine us, or seize our licence, else we won't get off our phones. A quiet sunset can become a frenzied hunt for the perfect selfie spot before the sun goes down. Apparently, we can no longer focus.

Practical tips for office-goers

- Always treat your work as a means to your own growth, not just as a task delivered in exchange for your salary.
- Handle even the smallest of roles as if it were the most important one you ever had.
- Concentrate on the job at hand and switch off from the rest of the world when you are executing it.

Not focusing on the person you are having dinner with, and recurrently checking your phone instead, is plain bad manners. However, when you can't focus *at work*, it has a larger implication. You are then, willingly, part of a conspiracy to embrace mediocrity. And if it becomes a part of your subconscious, you are doing yourself significant damage.

If you want to be good, or even great, at your work, you have to listen to Vivekananda when he makes this point: which is, whether you are repairing a computer, writing an article, tending to your garden, examining a patient, playing badminton, serving a burger, standing guard at a border outpost – *whatever* the nature of the work you are doing, *devote your whole life to it for the time being.*

When we handle work in a fragmented, half-engaged, distracted space, it reflects in the final result. So much is left half-done, so much has to be redone, because we work on autopilot while our mind is engaged in multiple other things. 'Work *is* worship.' When you work, you have to concentrate on your job at hand and switch off from the rest of the world.

While at work, Vivekananda reiterates two basics: focus and respect.

The manner in which the mystic Pavhari Baba, whom Vivekananda had described as an ideal yogi, went about his work, reflects the two basics of focus and respect. Speaking of him, Vivekananda once said:

> *One of his great peculiarities was his entire absorption at the time in the task at hand, however trivial. The same amount of care and attention was bestowed in cleaning a copper pot as in the worship of Shri Raghunathji, he himself being the best example of the secret he once told us of work: 'The means should be loved and cared for as if it were the end itself.'*

This is very close to Karma Yoga, but you need not look at it as religious or monastic. Even if you are agnostic, or utterly disinterested in the monastic reflexes of both Pavhari Baba and Vivekananda, following the yogi and the monk's views on work will help you be more organized, earn greater respect, and deliver better results in anything you take up.

Would you, for instance, give the same care and attention to cleaning a copper pot as in the worship of the deity? What thoughts come to mind when you visualize this?

This is what comes to my mind – a recap of so many previous thoughts:

- *'No work is petty.'*
- *Doing well the duty nearest to us.*
- *Not grumbling at 'the little thing'.*
- *'Do not think of anything beyond.'*

It all reflects the same core thought, worded differently. Essentially, it is a mindset that may seem abstract or other-worldly from a distance, but is very practical, once you get down to understanding it.

'Do not be afraid of small beginnings'

Part of the first dilemma at work is about *what* a good fit for us is. What's 'good enough'? Is this below our benchmark or too tough for us? Do we wait for what's really cool-sounding or do we head out and take what comes our way first? Do we do what we feel excited about or what is supposed to be safer and steadier? It's almost an extension of the 'course or college' dilemma that the Delhi University aspirant faces each year.

My career at the outset was so inconsequential that it would barely register as a blip on the horizon. At that time, I watched with amazement how people who (I thought) were not half as good as me were heading out into 'national' visibility, while there I was, struggling to break out of my mofussil branding. I wondered if I was in the right line; if I should not step out of it and strive for a more stable line of work, whether I had overrated my abilities, whether this much slogging for such little money was heading anywhere. Vivekananda held me back from panicking as he explained:

> *Do not be afraid of small beginnings, great things come afterwards. Be courageous.*

In your early years, this small lesson can be a great anchor. We can easily make the mistake of equating small beginnings with our own smallness, for want of a better word. We can feel inferior in comparison to friends, relatives and peers who have the skill and fortune to have moved far beyond small beginnings. We can feel defeated at the very outset, lose faith in ourselves, and let go of the larger picture as we absorb the disappointment of the 'small beginning'. A very junior position, an opening with a brand that is far smaller than the one we had hoped to start out with, a struggling start-up that we keep our fingers crossed about – there are so many 'small beginnings' we may experience. But that's all right.

Vivekananda softly nudges and reminds us not to panic, to not lose courage, and to trust, for 'great things come afterwards'.

Dealing with Failures and Setbacks

ABRAHAM LINCOLN WAS ESSENTIALLY right when he said that almost anyone can handle adversity, and that to test a man's character, you must give him power.

However, all of us aren't tested equally on this parameter. Many of us will probably have to handle loss, failure and frustration, but not all of us will be tested to see if a surge of unexpected power short-circuits our humility and our common sense. 'Almost anyone can handle adversity' may perhaps be accurate – but my modification to the original thought is that just *how* you handle it is what differentiates you from being 'almost anyone' else.

The man who can handle adversity with class will not fall short when power comes his way; the player who starts by being gracious in his defeats will, in all probability, be humble in victory, too.

Since adversity and failure are statistically and logically, greater certainties in life than vertigo-inducing heights of success, we may as well spend some time and energy honing our reflexes to deal with them. There is a certain class to handling conventional 'failure' without losing your mind – or your basics.

Earlier in life, I was fixated with how 'almost everyone' who is anyone in Indian epics handled failure. Ram's story becomes a *story* from the moment he opts to *not* handle power to keep his father's word. Almost all the key episodes that one read about were essentially from the point when he was about to be crowned king, to the point when he is back from exile and finally crowned. Ninety per cent of what we understand

and celebrate of his story is based on the period in which he handles exile and adversity, not power.

The story of the Pandavas is about losing their kingdom and living in exile, about their wanderings in exile, the *agyatvaas*, and finally about the war at Kurukshetra. The story centres around gaining the kingdom – about establishing and handling power. But how much do we recall about that handling? And does that even matter? Would it have defined them more than their handling of adversity did? Is there anything that Arjun did *after* the battle was won (and the kingdom attained) which defines what he was, what he stood for, to us?

Karna's story is about recurrent humiliation and failure with a few patches to offset that, and of final defeat on the battlefield, while the narrative on Abhimanyu is of an inspirational effort, but one that he did not live to see. Eklavya's story is one of great sincerity, but he, too, 'failed' in achieving what he set out to be – an exceptional archer – as he voluntarily sacrificed his thumb. There is no conventional career 'success' that any of them have, proportionate to what they invested. Yet their stories have a certain recall, because of *what* they were and *how* they approached the questions they faced, and not because of the positions they held. In contrast, although a Nakul or Sehdev had infinitely more time and opportunity to handle power, being on the side that won and then ruled did not make either their lives or their characters more aspirational. I, at least, cannot recall much about them.

What has all this got to do with Vivekananda, or with your life or mine?

Essentially, this: your friendly neighbourhood astrologer may or may not be able to trace out a '*rajyog*' or a golden phase in your life charts, but there's a 99 per cent chance that he will apprise you of the inevitability of the next 'difficult period'. Every single time someone's seen my horoscope, the crux of it has been: the near future is always a 'phase of tension', but in the 'long run', all is well. That long run is a very elusive entity. Maybe that's your story too. We will have complex periods more often – sometimes far more often than we'd wish – than we will have golden ones. Not to talk about the many times when we will probably fail and struggle and be stuck and helpless.

We may tend to crash when that happens, even need sustenance and support, maybe sympathy. We will perhaps need shoulders to cry on, peers to agree at the injustice life is doling out to us, people to reassure us that better times are just around the corner. Paulo Coelho too will pitch in to assure us that once we make up our minds to achieve something, the Universe will conspire to bring it to us.

But what if we didn't need any of this – the support, the reassurance?

What if we could embrace adversity and be comfortable with all the phases of life that can go wrong, or are going wrong? What if we are okay with not having as much money, influence, friends and dreams fulfilled as we'd have liked to have? What if we could laugh it off, rather than always wait, like undertrials awaiting a decision on a bail application, for the tough times to go and the good ones to finally start?

Life brings more failures than success.
Learn to be comfortable with them.

Vivekananda celebrated failure. He treated it with the same disdain that he treated success. He existed in a space where neither was more desirable than the other.

- Come good, come evil, both of you welcome, both of you my play.
- All time is yours, there is no indecent haste. Everything will come right if you are pure and sincere.

Vivekananda practically celebrated failure. Actually, he treated it with the same disdain that he treated success. To him, neither was more desirable than the other.

> *Come good, come evil, both of you welcome, both of you my play. I have no good to attain, no ideal to clench up to, no ambition to fulfil; I, the diamond mine, am playing with pebbles, good and evil… If the universe tumbles around my ears, what is that to me? I am Peace that passeth understanding; understanding only gives us good or evil. I am beyond, I am peace.*

On other occasions, he was more direct in his communication. There is fundamental simplicity in this:

> *Neither money pays, nor fame, nor learning; it is character that can cleave through adamantine walls of difficulties.*

You or I may not yet be 'the peace that passeth understanding', but we can at least try to absorb a thought as direct as this. When I do absorb it, my response is: I'm okay with not really having much money or fame. I'm okay with being of no great intellectual ability either – even at this moment, I am struggling to convey what a mind as evolved as Vivekananda's meant to say, probably with huge losses in transmission as I attempt to transmit what little I grasped of it. Life can go on, without losing much of its meaning, even if we are not very blessed with money, fame or learning. We can still find strength within us to manage the battles that it brings our way. Even if there is none else standing alongside.

As he summed it up:

> *Do not care for anybody to help you. Is not the Lord greater than all human help?*

When you keep 'Neither money pays…' and 'Do not care for…' as reference points, then, even as the years go by, you don't have too many panic attacks in tough situations. That's because you do not feel lost if you do not have money or fame to define you. When time tires you out and when you feel you have missed the bus of the standard benchmarks of success, you pause and take a minute out to read through other reminders that Vivekananda has sent your way.

- *Upon ages of struggle a character is built. Be not discouraged.*
- *All time is yours, there is no indecent haste. Everything will come right if you are pure and sincere.*

Of the people who followed Vivekananda from an early age is a name I have read a lot about in other contexts – Subhas Chandra Bose. I had a sense of déjà vu when I came across this line in his writings:

'I was barely fifteen when Vivekananda entered my life. Then there followed a revolution within and everything was turned upside down.'

Over time, when I had read in detail about both of them, I found a sense of Vivekananda's thoughts reflected in Bose's actions. Bose's life is a story of never-ending 'failures'. In his book, *The Indian Pilgrim*, he recounts that after he was accused of being part of the group of students who had manhandled a professor at the Presidency College in Calcutta, the principal sent for him and said, 'Bose, you are the most troublesome man in the college. I suspend you.'

His response? 'I said "Thank you" and went home.' Some days later, he writes, 'Lying on the bunk in the train at night, I reviewed the events of the last few months. My educational career was at an end, and my future was dark and uncertain. But I was not sorry – there was not a trace of regret in my mind for what I had done.'

The young man whose 'educational career was at an end', some years later cleared the Indian Civil Service exam. Then he resigned from it, for his conscience would not allow him to serve an imperial government ruling over his fellow countrymen. He went on to become the youngest mayor of Calcutta and embarked on a political career. But there were more failures coming his way. In 1939, he resigned yet again, this time from the presidency of the Indian National Congress, for the Mahatma and his associates held views very divergent from his on how the Congress was to move ahead.

By 1940, Bose was not an ICS officer, neither a powerful politician. He was merely an expelled Congress leader, in prison. Did anyone come to help him out? Did he rely on money or fame? Was he discouraged?

Now, where was Bose in 1942?

In Europe, asking Mussolini and Hitler to help India build her own army of independence. By 1944, when the German advance eastwards ground to a halt in Russia, he was addressing soldiers in Singapore and elsewhere, as he reshaped the Indian National Army into his own force. A year later, in 1945, he was facing yet another failure, as the INA and the Japanese withdrew after military defeats on the Burma-India frontier.

He did not change his basic reflexes till his last day, irrespective of whether they brought immediate reward or extended struggle.

Do our careers have greater challenges than his? He faced an academic crisis; a professional crisis of conscience; political fame and then hostility; military effort and then defeat. There were many who would have done better than him at every point. He could have been another student who topped Presidency College that year, or another candidate who joined the ICS and came back to a powerful posting in India, or another Congress leader who became president, or been a military leader who was on the winning side in 1945 on that frontier. Yet, he *did* matter, he did live a life worth talking about even today.

'Upon ages of struggle' a character *was* built. It was character that 'cleaved through adamantine walls of difficulties' repeatedly. And a part of how he handled everything, at least to my mind, began with that teenage 'revolution within' when 'everything was turned upside down'.

Should we give up on the struggles we face so quickly? Let us dig in.

Is Bose too romantic or flamboyant to be relatable? If so, let us look at a more practical, corporate example.

Head honchos sometimes face unexpected exile in the corporate world. Lee Iacocca would have thought he had done something of consequence when he traversed the journey from assistant sales manager to the president of the Ford Motor Company. In 1978, Ford earned a $2 billion profit. How did the year go for Iacocca? He was fired. Did that bring about a long mulling over injustice, loss of fame, money, and so on? Not quite. To cut a long story short, by 1992, he was the president, CEO and chairman of Chrysler, after having enabled the *other* auto giant – Ford's competitor – to turn around a collapsing business and regain relevance.

My takeaway from Vivekananda's approach is this – let us not be desperate for coronations and scared of exiles. Let us not be dependent on help from others, or be easily discouraged. Let us not rate acquiring money and fame too highly, nor mourn their loss too much.

My takeaway from Vivekananda's approach is this – let us not be desperate for coronations and scared of exiles. Let us not be dependent on help from others, or be easily discouraged.

Let us be in 'no indecent haste'. Let us not take our career ahead like a rush hour boarding of the Metro or a bus, pushing, shoving, elbowing, always worried about getting ahead of the rest. Better to miss a few buses, and let a few trains go by. It is okay to reach a little late, wait a few minutes extra at the traffic signal, and let others go ahead. Let those who push and shove better than you get whatever it is that they so desperately desire ahead of you. Do not shove back unless in self-defence. How does it matter? Is it worth it?

Let there be no indecent haste. 'Everything will come right if you are pure and sincere.' And of course, if you merit it. Remind yourself of it when you are tempted to rush in, to elbow others aside, physically or metaphorically, or when you feel left behind on the career escalator. No Indecent Haste.

If nothing else, there's a certain class to it.

Beyond the world of Vivekananda, Bose and Iacocca – big people, big issues, somewhat floating above our more mundane world of punching cards, salary slips and annual appraisals – there are other more practical takeaways when you put together all the points Vivekananda has made. I will assemble a few here once again, to help explain the inference I am drawing from it.

- *Even the greatest fool can accomplish a task if it be after his heart. But the intelligent man is he who can convert every work into one that suits his taste. No work is petty. He indeed is intelligent who notices this and succeeds in making all work truly great.*
- *By doing well the duty which is nearest to us, the duty which is in our hands now, we make ourselves stronger...We find ourselves in the position for which we are fit, and if one has some capacity above another, the world will find it out too...*

- *He who grumbles at the little thing that has fallen to his lot to do, will grumble at everything. Always grumbling, he will lead a miserable life. But that man who does his duty as he goes, putting his shoulder to the wheel, higher and higher duties will fall to his share.*
- *Do not be afraid of small beginnings, great things come afterwards. Be courageous.*
- *Neither money pays, nor fame, nor learning; it is character that can cleave through adamantine walls of difficulties.*
- *Upon ages of struggle a character is built. Be not discouraged.*
- *All time is yours, there is no indecent haste. Everything will come right if you are pure and sincere.*

How do we apply the basics of all these things he is saying?

You've worked well, very well, you think. You feel, genuinely, that you deserve the hiring, hike or promotion ahead of most people in your peer group.

And you don't get it.

It may appear to you that this happened because they have better 'boss management' skills, better references, or that they pitched their case to HR smarter but not entirely accurately; they are just sweet-talking their way into things and nobody seems to realize that. Or that the system is biased against you.

It could be any, or all, or none of these. You may be completely right, partly right, or completely wrong in your assessment. Irrespective of which of these it is, you will not feel good about the situation.

Now, there is another way to look at such a situation:

If someone is *actually* not good enough for a position they have been upgraded to, that is the worst thing to happen to them. There is no reason whatsoever for you to feel envious.

And if the person *is* good enough, a reality check is coming your way.

Essentially, such an angst-ridden situation can head either way:

- **Possibility A:** The individual will prove to be incapable of handling the role assigned. Higher positions immediately and unforgivingly magnify our strengths and weaknesses both and the stint will therefore not be a sustainable one. Future growth opportunities for such an individual will be impacted by the display of competence – or rather the lack of it. You just have to take a look at how many sporting careers lasted only one season, or how many actors gave up after a series of projects that they were unable to pull off. Getting something *before* you can deliver is not always a gift; it is on the contrary, often a self-goal, since later on, the inability to deliver at that point continues to influence how systems assign you roles later. As Vivekananda said: 'No man can long occupy satisfactorily a position for which he is not fit.'
- **Possibility B:** The individual will actually prove to be reasonably competent, and if you see it objectively, you will realize that the people who took the call to install the person in that post were not without basis. The person will evolve, display maturity, and handle the role well. And you will have to give the devil his or her due. Your option could be then to show similar maturity in your response, to take a balanced look at whether there are things the person perhaps had done better than you would have, and why. This learning then becomes an investment into your *own* future, and you, hopefully, look to build on the basics afresh, rather than expend energy in angst or envy. Good sporting teams, when beaten soundly by an opponent, take time to study the techniques adopted by the better team, and if feasible, look to adopt them as well. You can do the same when beaten professionally,

> can you not? Here is what Vivekananda had said: 'By doing well the duty which is *nearest* to us, the duty which is in our hands *now*, we make ourselves stronger; and improving our strength in this manner we may even reach a state in which it shall be our privilege to do the most coveted and honoured duties in life and in society.'

Maybe it was *you* who had not yet reached that state? Isn't that a possibility?

To repeat: There is no point in burning yourself out emotionally over who has got a role ahead of you. You could even have run for the US presidential elections, and may have got a greater number of total votes, but lost, given that a majority of the popular vote does not always translate into an electoral college majority. Without significant exception, however, the Vivekananda rule holds: 'No man can long occupy satisfactorily a position for which he is not fit.' If the individual is fit for that position, it was deserved, and your anger is misplaced; if the individual is not fit for that role – or does not evolve when placed in it – the decision is misplaced, and it will unroll sooner than later.

'Long', of course, is a key word, and it tests our patience. But work, our career – whether in business, cinema, journalism, sport, or medicine – is always a test match, not a T20, and we must know when to watch the pitch and when to bat aggressively. Patience is a career skill, not a weakness. Again, Vivekananda: 'No indecent haste'.

Competition and Rewards

We are all apt to think too highly of ourselves. We determine what our duties are to a much larger extent than we are willing to admit. Competition arouses envy, and kills the kindliness of the heart.

We live in a delusional bubble. We think work is a two-dimensional plane. Work well (and 95 per cent of us think we have worked very well every single year) and be rewarded.

Good work = good money and quick growth.

Perhaps it comes from the simplicity of the years of studying. Work harder in preparing = score more marks. Train harder = get into the college basketball team.

But the real world isn't always like that. A thousand things step in to influence how things turn out for an individual. And you don't have to decode the Gita to see that.

Across the world, a 'recession year' will see salaries dip and roll back, something which has little to do with how good or bad any one individual's work is. People doing a very good job in a badly managed system can be tossed out one day because the organization shuts down. Or you could be doing a very good job in a very well-managed organization and *still* be tossed out because of situations that neither you nor your organization could have anticipated. The year 2020 will long be remembered by millions across the globe who were handed out pink slips as the coronavirus pandemic ensured that most economies had a meltdown in fast forward. How well you had worked in 2019 didn't really matter – there were no rewards to be handed out in 2020. In many organizations, *keeping* your job was the reward for having done a great job.

So good work in year one = great rewards in year two? In theory, yes, but in the real world, you don't know.

Equally, despite very mediocre work, people have held on to safe and steady jobs for years, because the collective pulling power of their teams and brands easily hides their inadequacy. Or because they are in a monopoly market or their organization is a state-run entity with no alternative for the consumer to engage with.

A boom year can see salaries jump more than we merited because of competitive hiring; a bad year where competition is laying off half the staff can see you happy just to have a stable CTC. A great officer in the army could lose out on his life's ambition of heading a command because he retired just before a slot fell vacant. On the other hand, an Eisenhower, who was promoted to Lt Col in 1936, can get the acting rank of a four-star general in 1943 *because* it is wartime. A skilled and lucky Wehrmacht soldier could well have moved up four ranks in a year in the 1940s as he replaced casualties at senior levels in rapid succession on the Russian front, but peacetime isn't likely to bring such growth for a German soldier today, no matter how brilliant or courageous he may be.

Your work and your skill is one element of your *visible* growth. It is the most important element, for sure, but not the *only* element. Understand, recognize and accept that.

And yes, like it or not, destiny will play its part. From the armed forces to politics to sport, there is no dearth of unanticipated movements in careers. But *once* destiny has played its part in placing you somewhere – or in placing someone else where you would have wanted to be – a second set of dynamics play out.

Merely occupying a chair is not a welcome development if the occupant is not fit for it, since all it does is to bring a sharper spotlight on one's deficiencies. There is, therefore, little point in grudging another's growth; it's far better to focus on what is in one's hands.

Vivekananda explains clearly how you need to converse with yourself in uncomfortable situations, something which we have referred to earlier as well.

- *No man can long occupy satisfactorily a position for which he is not fit. By doing well the duty which is nearest to us, the duty which is in our hands now, we make ourselves stronger; and improving our strength in this manner we may even reach a state in which it shall be our privilege to do the most coveted and honoured duties in life and in society.*
- *We find ourselves in the position for which we are fit, and if one has some capacity above another, the world will find that out too. He who grumbles at the little thing that has fallen to his lot, will grumble at everything. Always grumbling he will lead a miserable life. But that man who does his duty as he goes, putting his shoulder to the wheel, higher and higher duties will fall to his share…*

The world does not have a perfect, mechanical system to give you exactly what you merit. The system assessing you to hire, assign a task, promote or award a bonus *will* be subjective. Equally, you *will* have a higher degree of subjectivity in looking at your own case. It is neither right nor wrong – it is just how things are. As long as the world is inhabited by people, there will be opinions, and differences of opinion as well.

The question is what to do when the difference of opinion works *against* you. Nobody has a problem with an umpire's decision on a 50-50 call when it has gone in your favour. When it has gone against you, however, you are more likely to question the entire manner in which such umpiring decisions are taken.

What do we miss in those angry moments? The fact that umpiring is never perfect. And the fact that errors go *both* ways – for you and against you – and it almost always evens out in the long run for almost all batsmen. But there's no point smashing the bat into the ground and swearing and cribbing to the universe when you have to walk back to the pavilion even if you didn't edge the ball. It happens to *everyone.* If you're a really good batsman, it won't destroy your career. If it is enough to destroy it, then, frankly, you didn't have much of a career in the first place.

What does Vivekananda's life have to do with this, you may ask?

First, when you get angry, you make a mess of things. At 25, I did not get this point he made; at 45, I could not but agree with it.

- *I have been asked many times how we can work if we do not have the passion we generally feel for work. I also thought in that way years ago, but as I am growing older, getting more experience, I find it is not true. The less passion there is, the better we work. The calmer we are, the better for us, and the more the amount of work we can do. When we let loose our feelings we waste so much energy, shatter our nerves, disturb our minds, and accomplish very little work... It is the calm, forgiving, equitable, well-balanced mind that does the greatest amount of work.*

Calm. Forgiving. Equitable. Well-balanced.

As they say so often on Twitter, Let That Sink In.

The description is closer to that of a monk's mindspace than that of someone fighting workplace battles, but there is truth to it. The calmer we are, the better for us. Let us not shatter our nerves and disturb our minds simply in emphasizing the injustice being done to us. It does not make us capable of doing more or better work. In the long run, it often becomes counterproductive.

Every instance of short-lived success, whether of a politician, a cine star or a sportsman, has served to reiterate the point he made – *no man can long occupy a position for which he is not fit*. 'Long' is relative and a technicality, of course, as we have discussed; I tend to read it more in the sense of no man can have *a lasting impact* on a position for which he is not fit. Many chief ministers and prime ministers and presidents may have 'long occupied a position' but it is unlikely that their tenures will be studied at a B-School of global repute as an empowering or administrative role model. Others have brief stints that leave us wondering what they may have not done if only they had a longer crack at the job.

So let's not grumble at the 'little things' that come our way. In the bigger scheme of life, *all* things are little things. You can run a big thing horrendously or do a small thing well; the latter is not inferior to the former simply on account of scale. Millions to command or billions to spend may not necessarily be ours, but to rewind to Vivekananda's thinking, *if we have some capacity above the other, the world will find that out too.* That is a universal truth.

But a word of caution before we rush ahead.

Vivekananda is saying: If we *have* some capacity above the other.

He is *not* saying: If we *think* we have some capacity above the other.

You must objectively assess if you have such a capacity. If not, you must acquire it. And then you must work to build and sustain it, till the point it is no longer a matter of conjecture, opinion or approximation, but a given, accepted fact that you *have* it. The fact that you *feel* or you *think* you have it is neither here nor there. The Universe, regrettably, does not conspire to bring us rewards just because we feel we merit them.

So, if we think we have some capacity above others, and we think it is not being appreciated, let us not waste our energy in cynicism, angst, and generally complaining about life's injustices. Instead, let us put our shoulder to the wheel.

A monk's mindspace for work

- It is the calm, forgiving, equitable, well-balanced mind that does the greatest amount of work.
- The less passion there is, the better we work. The calmer we are, the better for us, and the more the amount of work we can do.
- As I grow older I find that I look more and more for greatness in little things.

– Vivekananda

Virat Kohli was working on his fitness, his batting, and his skills well before he was anywhere close to the cricketing icon he is today. Nelson Mandela was doing what he could, fighting the battle at hand, spending decades in prison, before he became the global inspiration that we know him as. Field marshals and admirals who are studied in the history of warfare today – Napoleon, Nelson, Rommel, Montgomery, Eisenhower, or Manekshaw – were, if you go back down their career track, doing more than they needed to do as lieutenants, or as captains. They were putting their shoulder to the wheel, they were *doing well the duty that was nearest* to them. The story is no different in sports, politics, management, science or in cinema.

Stop competing with others. Stop tracking their growth. Stop simmering in angst when you feel you have a raw deal and others have it all handed on a platter. Find your satisfaction from the *quality* of the work you do, not the *scale* of it. Your team may be small, your book may not have so many readers, your documentary may not be watched by millions, you may be a junior officer commanding 15 men, not a general commanding thousands. That is all right. In fact, you may do well to read *The Peter Principle* to get a sense of the fact that many people doing things at a bigger *scale* at a more 'senior' position are not necessarily doing a *better* job. They may well stagnate where they are, a couple of ranks above you, because they have come to their 'level of incompetence', i.e., the point at which they cannot be given greater responsibility. You can work on yourself and look to move four ranks from where you are so that when *you* are where they are today, the story is not repeated.

My take on work:

Stop competing with others. Stop tracking their growth. Stop simmering in angst when you feel you have a raw deal and others have it all handed on a platter. Find your satisfaction from the quality of the work you do, not the scale of it.

On the point of greater scale or greater seniority not necessarily being equal to greater skill, or greater satisfaction, something that Vivekananda said in his later years may help give perspective.

> *As I grow older I find that I look more and more for greatness in little things... Anyone will be great in a great position. Even the coward will grow brave in the glare of the footlights. The world looks on!*

More and more the true greatness seems to me that of the worm doing its duty silently, steadily, from moment to moment and hour to hour.

We tend to applaud enthusiastically those who respond grandly in high visibility situations, and to ignore, or take for granted, those who discharge their duties silently and diligently. The video of a policeman running after a criminal will go viral; the crowd goes ecstatic when a batsman delivers a last-ball boundary; whereas the nurse in a children's ward in a village hospital who goes from one bed to another, investing all of herself into patients who cannot write long posts of gratitude for her on social media once discharged, is not very likely to be 'in the glare of the footlights'.

Vivekananda challenges your conventional reflexes – what you applaud and what you aspire to be. He makes you question whether the grandeur of shining medals, award ceremonies, and the other glitter that high-visibility roles bring is the only thing worth respecting, or worth emulating.

Even if it is unsettling, think about it.

To recap – work on yourself. Remind yourself, over and over:

We find ourselves in the position for which we are fit, and if one has some capacity above another, the world will find that out too.

Work to build that capacity. Once you have it, trust that the world will find that out, too.

What can be a simpler work philosophy?

Dealing with Hostility

IN YOUR INITIAL YEARS, *before* you gain some degree of relevance or responsibility, you will probably receive a fair amount of unsolicited wisdom. Some of it will be well-intentioned and will help you understand the process, the people, and the basics of your profession. Some will be random opinion and spicy gossip which will come your way depending on how keen you are to receive more of it.

Once you *are* relevant, responsible, or in a position of authority, you are more likely to face less friendly stuff. You may have to deal with your share of giggly gossip or office politics, while in some instances you will face active hostility, resistance, and slander as well. It can trip you if are overly sensitive, or if you are very concerned with what people think or say about you.

In the first and third parts of this book, I have reiterated that Vivekananda taught me to stand by myself, without looking for peer support, and ignoring standard social expectations. Many of those reflexes naturally made their way into the responses to pressure or hostility in work situations as well.

Vivekananda's thoughts on this subject were those he typically had when responding to public opinion – largely one of indifference:

> *Let the world say what it chooses, I shall tread the path of duty... Otherwise, if one has to attend day and night to what this man says or that man writes, no great work is achieved in this world.*

My takeaway was that even if one took away the grandeur from this – the 'path of duty', the bit about 'great work' – even then, at a very basic level, from deciding who should open the batting to how to promote your film or what to place on the front page of a paper, no coherent work is done if you are paying attention day and night to 'what this man says or that man writes'.

Absorbing, ignoring, or reflecting on what is said is an important part of handling work. Pay too little attention to all feedback and you are likely to live in an ivory tower, and not be sensitive and receptive. Pay too much attention to every opinion around you and you may as well hold a vote on every decision you take. But if you do that, why should you be given the role of a decision-maker in the first place? Robin Sharma makes the point that 'Leadership is not a popularity game. It's not about doing what's easy. It's about doing what's right. We are too bothered about being judged,' and about wondering what this or the other says or writes.

If you cannot take unpopular calls, leadership roles aren't your thing at work.

What are the larger takeaways on this subject for someone who wants to handle work through the prism of Vivekananda's basic philosophy?

One, sniping and comments are as integral to work as sledging is to sport or propaganda is to warfare. The cricketers who seem immune to verbal drama tend to have longer careers than the ones who have a short fuse and love to 'give it back'. Kids who are the quickest to react are more fun for school bullies. Disengagement and ignoring such things is not weakness, but a means of conserving energy.

> The names of those who will wish to injure us will be legion. But is not that the surest sign of our having the truth? The more I have been opposed, the more my energy has always found expression.
>
> – Vivekananda

Two, don't wear your heart on your sleeve and allow yourself to be instigated or egged on to stupid responses that you will not be proud of later. Hyper-emotionalizing all battles, disagreements and bad days at the workplace is a very taxing model of functioning.

Vivekananda does not stress about hostility directed at you. He looks at it as a vindication of having taken a stand:

> *The names of those who will wish to injure us will be legion. But is not that the surest sign of our having the truth? The more I have been opposed, the more my energy has always found expression.*

He practically relished confrontation. All of us, however, do not have his energy. We have to think about when to engage and when to avoid. We have to assess when feedback or criticism is worth our analysis and time, and when it is something we can do nothing about – and nothing is exactly what one should do. In taking this call, Vivekananda has a very effective lesson to offer. I call it the 'Mr Hudson test'.

The Mr Hudson Test

This is a very specific lesson I took away from a letter Vivekananda wrote; one that has taught me to filter what to react to and what to ignore. It is applicable across life, but I apply it most often to the workplace, and for that reason, it finds itself in this portion of the book. Despite that, it is by no means just a work lesson.

The lines that I underlined, highlighted and circled from *The Letters of Swami Vivekananda* were these:

> *Every undertaking must pass through a lot of obstacles. Truth triumphs if only one pursues a peaceful course. I have no need to reply to what a Mr Hudson has spoken against me. In the first place, it is unnecessary, and secondly, I shall be bringing myself down to the level of people of Mr Hudson's type. Are you mad? Shall I fight from here with one Mr Hudson? Through the Lord's grace, people who are far above Mr Hudson in rank listen to me with veneration.*

It is a passing line in a letter, where Vivekananda is responding to his disciples flagging off criticism about him from a gentleman, presumably a Mr Hudson, and urging him to write a note of rebuttal. It enabled me to take a lifetime of decisions when caught in a dilemma. The dilemma, of course, is how to respond to upfront criticism and flak as well as the below-the-belt personal attacks.

Now, generally speaking, I have tried to keep in mind the very sensible point made by Theodor Leschetizky:

> *We learn much from the disagreeable things people say, for they make us think; whereas the good things only make us glad.*

However, beyond a point, the disagreeable things said by people do not just make us think, but also irritated, upset and furious. Should we, therefore, react to them by simply ignoring them? It is tempting, but then we will never correct ourselves in any space, even if the criticism is genuine and legitimate. As Vivekananda wrote elsewhere, we are all tempted to think too highly of ourselves. By assuming that all that we do is grand and desirable, we will stay fixated in the behaviour, thoughts and reflexes we grew up with while being needlessly proud of our 'personality'.

Should we then search our soul for the motive behind every critical comment we receive? Should we change our life patterns for every individual who does not take a fancy to our way of living? But do we owe people that, more so when much of the flak today is anonymous, or, like a WhatsApp forward, its origin is pretty much untraceable? Will the critics do the same for *our* feedback? Where do we include innuendo, gossip, trolling and grapevine opinion – is it even to be given the status of 'feedback' when the holder of an opinion can't give it to your face? And what about people generally not liking our face? Do we change that, too?

What do we look to be? Obstinate, narcissistic and dismissive of all criticism, or petrified people-pleasers, spending sleepless nights when we hear unflattering commentary about ourselves?

There are no easy answers to these questions.

Here is where Mr Hudson can help. Let me explain how.

My first takeaway was this:

I have no need to reply to what a Mr Hudson has spoken against me.

The more I thought about this, the less and less frequently I began to respond to remarks, opinions or snide commentary made about me. Over time, I realized there is usually no *need* to reply. When something is spoken against us, very rarely is it worthy of a response. On most occasions, when we react, we don't do so because it was *required* – we react because we are irked, or our ego is hurt, or our 'honour' demands that we counter this nonsense.

But we don't *need* to.

Twenty years ago, when I looked at some of the battles I was getting into, I asked myself, did I really need to reply to a Mr Hudson? Today, every week, I see celebrities, or leaders, and their fans going hammer and tongs at each other on Twitter over some issue, and when I trace back where a particular spat began, I wonder – did X *need* to reply to what Y had said? What did it achieve? 'Mr Hudson' has the right to an opinion about you. Let him express it. What of it?

> **Uncertain about responding to flak?**
> **Time to take The Hudson Test.**
>
> When something is spoken against us, very rarely is it worthy of a response. On most occasions, when we react, we don't do so because it was required – we react because we are irked, or our ego is hurt, or our honour demands that we counter this nonsense. At such moments, take lessons from Vivekananda's 'Mr Hudson' letter. Filter out what merits your attention, and what should be simply ignored.

You may be important or relevant enough for Mr Hudson to hold an opinion about you and to make the effort to voice it. So what? The opposite of love is not hate; the opposite of love is indifference, right? By tearing into you, Mr Hudson has just displayed his inability to be indifferent to you. Do *you* find Mr Hudson relevant enough to have something to say about what he feels, even if it is about you? Why?

Disengage.

Most times, when I am tempted to counter a point, I go back to 1895, and I think of people urging Vivekananda to react to Mr Hudson's dim view of the monk from India. Vivekananda did not reply. Perhaps that was seen by some as a victory for

Mr Hudson's opinion. And then I remind myself that here I am, 125 years later, trying to write a book about Vivekananda, and I have not the least idea who Mr Hudson was and what issues he had with Vivekananda. Trolling, abusing or slandering someone is not victory, it is just angst-filled catharsis.

Let us live out our lives, to the best we can. Let us not rush to respond to every word spoken or written against us. Let our Mr Hudsons revel in our unwillingness to reply, let them see it as our inability to respond. And let them have a happy life on that account. What does it cost me? Or you?

The second part of this is even more educative.

> *Are you mad? Shall I fight from here with one Mr Hudson? Through the Lord's grace, people who are <u>far above Mr Hudson in rank</u> listen to me with veneration.*

From this, I drew out a rule of thumb that has served me well so far, and may be of some utility to you as well.

When I am being criticized, I try to understand the viewpoints of:

a) Mr Hudson,
b) those whom I see as his peers, and
c) those whom I think of as Mr Hudson's superiors, for want of a better word

For instance, let us say a Mr Hudson thinks that my writing is the worst he has ever seen, and I should quit this space altogether. I should be worried if that is an opinion shared widely. But if someone 'far above Mr Hudson in rank' – an accomplished author whom I have great regard for, for instance – has sent me a word of encouragement, then I may not quit writing just yet. I shall, however, also refrain from fighting with Mr Hudson. Or telling him what I think of *his* writing, for instance.

Cricket fans in India are hugely emotional and passionate about the game. After a bad series, there are many who feel that a few, or all the players, should give up the game altogether. On social media, every batsman who is going through a bad patch receives unsolicited advice on a range of issues, from his grip to his marriage.

If I were a batsman facing flak after a series where I generally failed, I would apply Vivekananda here. Perhaps Mr Hudson thinks I should change my grip, my stance, my coach, my attitude, or my special someone. Or all of these.

Some of the points may well be valid. Or it may be just a case of Mr Hudson being in a bad mood that day. Before I go about changing everything about my game, or announcing my early retirement, maybe I should also get a sense of the viewpoint of others who are 'far above Mr Hudson in rank' – people who have played 50-odd test matches, coached national teams, captained Team India, perhaps? If they, too, share a similar sentiment that I am not cut out to play at the international level, I should at least think long and hard about where I am heading. But if *they* think differently, and think my cricketing basics are sound, and, in fact, tell me to hang in there through this patch because they see me as the next Sachin or Dravid or Steve Smith – then I need to keep Mr Hudson away from charting out my life's path.

The 'rank' here is not about stature. As *The Peter Principle* often reminds us, merely being at a superior rank in a formal hierarchy is not always the same thing as being more capable. Rank here is more about whether Mr Hudson is *qualified* to give me wisdom. When I see a child who may have been laughed at by her class-fellows in the course of her musical journey get a standing round of applause from a jury that has artistes who have made a mark in music, I see that as a far-above-Mr-Hudson-in-rank moment for her. *Who* is assessing us is the key. Not in terms of what they *feel* about us, no, but in terms of how they are placed to assess us. Every parent may feel that their child is the next Lata Mangeshkar – but Lata Mangeshkar herself is far better placed than the parents to judge the child's musical abilities. In whatever we do – sing, act, write, run an office, design a car, style hair – many may have views, good or bad, about what we do and how we do it. We must, therefore, actively seek out the views of those *qualified* to actually comment on us, to point out our strengths and weaknesses, to have a reality check on our skills as well as our approach.

The views of the most *opinionated* must not become more important just because they are loud and shrill.

When I hear, for instance, that a Mr Hudson is of the opinion that I know nothing of how to run my office (this happens more often than you'd think, trust me), I check for two things:

a) Has Mr Hudson run an office, or anything, more efficiently, i.e., is he *qualified* to assess my managerial failings? Would he do it better if I handed it over to him tomorrow?
b) Over the past years, have the many people who have seen my work, and who run far bigger systems than I do, far more efficiently, and who are, therefore, far above me – as well as Mr Hudson – 'in rank', found my reflexes to be generally useless?

If the answer to both is no, then there is nothing more I intend to do about the issue, including thinking about it.

And so, when faced with questions about how to respond to criticism or feedback, I now, by reflex, think of Vivekananda's words and use them to draw up a filter.

- Is the current critic a random person, angry with the world in general, or with me, in particular, or is he a neutral person with good reason to say what he is saying? If the former, do I *need* to reply?
- Is this criticism a reiteration of what people better qualified than him or me also think? In other words, do those 'far above Mr Hudson in rank' *also* share his reservations (in which case I need to look carefully in the mirror), or is it that they, in fact, are saying the opposite?

So the test is this: if the critical views on both ends converge, I stop to reassess what I am doing wrong. However, if those 'far above Mr Hudson' think that I am generally doing okay, then I do not waste energy either lapsing into introspection or engaging with Mr Hudson when he speaks against me. If pressed to reply, to defend myself, I decline, and quote Vivekananda to those urging me on: *Are you mad?*

[PS: This extends beyond work as well. When it comes to religion or philosophy, I use Vivekananda himself as the benchmark. Living in a world where practising any religion is increasingly seen more as an exercise in meeting collective social benchmarks rather than a journey of individual discovery, if I am lectured on something I should or should not do, how to practise my faith, for instance, I turn to Vivekananda, '*far* above Mr Hudson in rank' so far as this field goes. And if I feel he would agree with what my reflex is, I pay no further attention to the advice.]

Finally, it was because of Vivekananda that:

- I learnt to view work without being chronically stressed, afraid or defensive.
- I learnt not to look at a career as something the world owes me. Things may or may not be 'big enough'; they may not be tailored to precisely fit my requirements.

A job role is not a restaurant menu or a bespoke suit – it isn't really meant to fit my preferences as the first priority. He reminds me that 'no work is petty' and warns me against turning into a habitual, lifelong grumbler.

- He reminds me to look inwards before blaming everyone around, especially when things aren't going my way.
- He teaches me to not grudge the growth of others and to understand that it is okay if someone has been unfairly moved ahead of me. No one can 'long occupy satisfactorily a position for which *he* is not fit' and 'we find ourselves in the position for which *we* are fit'. Essentially, I will either realize that my resentment was misplaced or the decision-makers will soon realize that they backed the wrong horse in the race.
- He tells me to stop philosophizing about the future or ranting about the past and to get down to doing things, to do 'the duty nearest to you', and to not do it half-heartedly, no matter how insignificant or marginal it may appear – this is a time-tested recipe for 'higher and higher duties' to come our way.
- He reiterates the importance of something we struggle with today – focus. When we are doing something, he reminds us, to 'not think of anything beyond'. That would include looking again and again at our phone notifications!
- He asks me to take it easy where the ego is concerned and when we succumb to the 'this-is-so-unfair-to-me' sentiment. He makes an obvious point that is often overlooked: 'We are all apt to think too highly of ourselves.' Remember that self-belief is good but self-delusion is not; find a middle point and be a neutral observer of your actions, once in a while.

- He asks me to not overrate passion beyond a point and to remember that 'the calmer we are, the more the amount of work we can do'.
- If you aren't quite the prodigy or the young achiever, or have had a quarter-life crisis at 25 or dread your 30th birthday since you haven't the salary or the rank or the role that matches other friends who post resort pictures on Instagram, it's okay. It is not the end of life. Have patience, he says. What is your due *will* come to you. Don't change into a lesser, shriller version of yourself because the calendar scared you. Remember, 'no indecent haste'.
- If you can't understand how to handle scolding, feedback, nasty emails, jibes, or trashing of your work, remind yourself that flak is integral to work. Instead of either melting under it or developing a rhino's hide and thinking you are God's gift to your workplace, find a middle point – filter your criticism. If it comes from qualified, neutral, skilled minds, give it weightage, and work on yourself. If it is prejudiced opinion or comment, apply the 'Mr Hudson Test' and do not waste energy decoding or responding to it.

Part 3

Dealing with Others

Loss, Grief, Acceptance

WHAT CAN I TELL you about death? It remains a paradoxical topic: always around us in a collective sense, yet pushed to the back of the mind in an individual sense.

Earlier in the book, we have explored how we often think about our own death. But like many others, my initial sense of fear of death was not about my own – since youth lets you be careless about such questions – but of those whom I cared about. Sometime in my early teens, I came across Samuel Johnson's extremely disturbing but extremely accurate point:

With regard to the sharpest and most melting sorrow, that which arises from the loss of those whom we have loved with tenderness, it may be observed, that friendship between mortals can be contracted on no other terms than that one must sometime mourn for the other's death: and this grief will always yield to the survivor one consolation proportionate to his affliction; for the pain, whatever it be, he himself feels, his friend has escaped.

This was depressing, even if incontestable.

The questions Johnson raised were genuinely scary. The way I saw it, life could then either be lived as a dry, dead, emotionless experience, or as an engaged but assuredly tragic one. At 17, these seemed to be two very bad choices for the rest of my life.

'Friendship between mortals can be contracted on no other terms than that one must some time mourn for the other's death'. So must all bonds end in mourning? And, therefore, the longer and deeper a bond between two people lasts, the greater the pain at either one finally dying will be. Does it mean that the one who lives longer will suffer more? Does it mean life is emotionally secure only when lived as a sanyasi, with nobody to care for, as Vivekananda wrote?

> *He who is alone is happy. Do good to all, like everyone, but do not love anyone. It is a bondage, and bondage brings only misery. Live alone in your mind – that is happiness. To have nobody to care for and never minding who cares for one is the way to be free.*

This reads well, but how does one *do* it? To have nobody to care for, to have nobody care for you: is this the way to be free, or the way to be a sociopath? It was all very unsettling.

Then, perhaps like for many of us, my introduction to mourning for the loss of a mortal friend came at the spot where my first pet lay buried.

This is how it happened.

My first pet was a puppy, a few days old, who was sitting quietly by a tree as I stepped out from a tennis court to walk back home one day. I was in Class XII and she was part of a litter of fox terriers being put up for adoption, but she had wandered off and settled by herself. She was utterly adorable. Holding her in my arms and walking home was the first major decision I took without parental approval. They unexpectedly abided with my decision. I took her to the vet, built a kennel for her, and generally understood how to take care of her even as both of us adjusted to each other's idiosyncrasies. For a year, I cared for her as I hadn't for anyone till then.

A year later, in college, I went off for a fortnight on my first NCC camp. As there were no mobile phones then, I had no contact with home during that period. The day I got off a dusty army truck outside home, Candy wasn't there scampering at the gate. I asked where she was, and was quietly taken to the spot where she lay buried.

She had fallen acutely ill for a week and passed away, despite the vet's efforts. My parents had thought it best to not inform me, to avoid disturbing me when I was all by myself. But for me it was shattering to realize that I could not even see her one last time, could not hold her in my arms before she was laid into her grave. We did not click truckloads of photos in those days and so I had barely a couple of photos of hers for memory's sake. I wept like a kid for a week. The memory is still sharp and painful.

With human loss, at least, there are occasionally some differences or grievances with those we lose, but a loving pet gives so much unconditionally that you live with guilt and regret for being the less deserving one in the relationship of affection, brief though it may have been.

I realized that all philosophical reading can't prepare you to handle death. I certainly wasn't prepared.

And that scared me badly. How would I handle the rest of life as it unfolded? Death seemed so frightening. I tried to understand the minds that seemed to be calm in the face of such an idea.

I noted the Buddha's transition from the curious prince who asked his charioteer what the funeral procession was all about to the tranquil philosopher who calmly asked a bereaved mother to bring a mustard seed from a home that had never seen death. I wondered how that level of understanding could be reached, without having to sit below a tree for so many days.

I picked up the Bhagvad Gita and tried to absorb Radhakrishan's commentary on death.

> *As the soul passes in this body through childhood, youth and age, even so is the taking on of another body. The sage is not perplexed by this.* (2.13)

But I wasn't a sage. I was in college. And I was massively perplexed. I tried, still, to comprehend the discussion:

Even if thou thinkest that the self is perpetually born and perpetually dies, even then, O Arjuna, thou shouldst not grieve. For to the one that is born, death is certain, and certain is birth for the one that has died. Therefore for what is unavoidable, thou shouldst not grieve. (2.26 & 27)

This track of the Gita has stayed with me for years; I will come back to it shortly. At that moment, however, I turned, once again, to Vivekananda.

Lessons in metaphysics

- The soul of man is a part of the eternal cosmic energy that exists, i.e., a part of God. It is beyond life and death. You were never born, and you will never die.
- Till we come to Vivekananda's state of being, we cannot be stoic in the face of loss. But we can at least have a sense of reassurance that the person we cared for has not been 'lost'. No one can be.

Sister Nivedita commented that on losing a good friend of his, Vivekananda had this to say:

Man must conquer this illusion and know that the dead are here beside us and with us, as much as ever. It is their absence and separation that are a myth.

That thought made me feel better, but the mind could not comprehend – *how* are they beside us? At other points, he explained the Gita's teaching in similar words.

- *Nature, body and mind go to death, not we. We neither go nor come. The man 'Vivekananda' is in nature, is born and dies; but the Self (soul) we see as 'Vivekananda' is never born and never dies. It is the eternal and unchangeable Reality.*
- *The soul of man is a part of the eternal cosmic energy that exists, i.e., a part of God. It is beyond life and death. You were never born, and you will never die. Then what is this birth and death that we see? These belong to the body, because the soul is omnipresent and eternal.*

In his letters, there was one written in 1895 to a Mrs Bull, who had lost her father. What he explained to her was a little simpler to comprehend.

- *Coming and going is all pure delusion. The soul never comes nor goes. Where is the place to which it shall go, when all space is in the soul?*
- *All souls that ever have been, are, or shall be, are all in the present tense... Because the idea of space does not occur in the soul, therefore all that were ours, are ours, and will be ours, are always with us. We are in them. They are in us...*
- *The cloud moves across the face of the moon, creating the illusion that the moon is moving. So nature, body, matter move on, creating the illusion that the soul is moving...Thus we find at last that instinct (or inspiration?) which men of every race, whether high or low, have had to feel, viz the presence of the departed about them, is true intellectually also.*
- *The whole secret is, then, that your father has given up the old garment he was wearing, and is standing where he was through all eternity. Will he manifest another such garment in this or any other world? I sincerely pray that he may not, until he does so in full consciousness. I pray that none may be dragged any whither by the unseen power of his own past actions. I pray that all may be free, that is to say, may know that they are free.*

Essentially, Vivekananda was saying to her that not only was there nothing to mourn in the passing away, he wished that the soul that has passed on does *not* return to take on another body. He therefore left me with the query that while we dearly want those who have left to return to us, is it perhaps better if they do not, so to say, manifest another such garment? Do we weep for *them*, or only for the place they wrench out of our lives? If we are less selfish, can we acquire the sagacity to understand the collective wisdom that is available to us – in my case, for instance, the Buddha, the Gita and Vivekananda – and to hope, instead, that the garment left behind is the last one our loved ones discard?

But how do we do it? What do we pluck out of this reservoir of advice and imbibe, beyond the flowery words and heavy concepts?

Finally, we never know till we are *really* tested, till we come face to face with it. I, too, didn't. Let me share with you how it went when I did.

Grief and Solace: My Tests of These Beliefs

VIVEKANANDA REMINDS US THAT, for you and for me, the generic question is, of course, one thing. But when someone we know, someone dear to us, dies, is when all the questions come to us with the most intensity:

> *What question has been asked a greater number of times, what idea has led men more to search the universe for an answer, what question is nearer and dearer to the human heart, what question is more inseparably connected with our existence, than this one, the immortality of the human soul? It has been the theme of poets and sages, of priests and prophets; kings on the throne have discussed it, beggars in the street have dreamt of it. The best of humanity have approached it, and the worst of men have hoped for it. The interest in the theme has not died yet, nor will it die so long as human nature exists. Various answers have been presented to the world by various minds. Thousands, again, in every period of history have given up the discussion, and yet the question remains fresh as ever. Often in the turmoil and struggle of our lives we seem to forget it, but suddenly some one dies — one, perhaps, whom we loved, one near and dear to our hearts is snatched away from us — and the struggle, the din and turmoil of the world around us, cease for a moment, and the soul asks the old questions 'What after this?' 'What becomes of the soul?'*

Yes, the struggle, the din of the world, does cease in that moment.

In 2018, when I stepped barefoot into the funeral pyre of my mother the day after her cremation, gathering up her mortal remains, all three of my reference points – Vivekananda, Buddha and the Gita – were going through my mind. I like to think that I was able to remember some of these lessons and stay focused on what it meant for *her* and not let it become entirely about me. I think keeping that perspective in my mind and heart enabled me to accept and absorb it with more calmness and stability than I would have expected. I was, in some ways, genuinely relieved for her – she was free of the frail health and dependency that she had endured for almost a year by then; she had left the garment behind. I did not know what would come after that, but I trusted, genuinely, that the world beyond would be a better place for her than where she had been.

The most intensely I experienced a collective sense of loss and grief amongst people I knew was in 2021. It is different from reading about collective loss, such as a plane crash or flood-induced devastation, where you regret what happened but aren't impacted individually because you don't know what someone is facing on a personal level.

The peak of the Covid-19 wave in the first half of 2021 – the 'second wave' for India, making the one in 2020 seem mild in comparison – was terrible.

One saw death all around. In a volume and recurrent intensity that was unprecedented.

Both my parents-in-law were admitted to the hospital on the same day, in Nagpur.

My mother-in-law passed away within 24 hours. My father-in-law survived the initial attack, stayed in the hospital for many days, and then came down with black fungus. We scampered to arrange the medication that we hoped would save his life at that point of time – Tocilizumab injections. Getting our hands on these was almost impossible, however, with great difficulty, we managed to do so, and were relieved and thankful. But as it turned out, that wasn't enough.

My father-in-law never came back from the hospital. My wife lost both her parents in just 45 days and couldn't even travel for the last rites.

A few days later, for almost an entire day, we struggled to arrange a hospital bed and oxygen for a colleague's mother in Lucknow while her oxygen levels dipped. By the time even the basics could be managed, she was beyond recovery. I still remember the messages being exchanged that day.

Another colleague, also in Lucknow, stopped trying to do all of this for her ailing father. The family gathered around him at home as they waited for the inevitable, taking comfort in the fact that he would at least pass away whilst being surrounded by his own people instead of dying in an isolated hospital bed. But the hospital queue followed even afterwards – at the cremation ground, they were given a token to wait. Number 126, if I remember correctly. I still remember the conversation about that. Some grieving relatives had opted to place bricks and cremate their loved ones on the road outside the cremation ground, given the long wait.

In Delhi, a young colleague accompanied her father to the hospital at 2 a.m., trailing an ambulance that had been arranged with some difficulty when breathing had become difficult for her father. This was after the oxygen concentrator arranged at home was no longer able to keep things going. When they reached the hospital, the ambulance crew informed her that it was all over – he had collapsed and could not be revived. While still in shock from the loss, four days later, she was at a cremation ground for a friend's mother's last rites, horrified by how people were jostling for space in order to give a dignified farewell to those who had meant so much to them. I don't think she has outgrown the traumatic memory of that week yet, or will even be able to, for a very long time.

There are more instances, but I will pause for now.

Amidst that unmanageable volume of hearing about human loss, I went back to find some sense in the pages of the Gita.

People were struggling with immense emotional impacts of the losses they were facing. There was so much loss that the default 'RIP', 'He/she is in a better place' or 'It is all God's will' did very little to bring anyone any sense of peace, or to even offer them the smallest degree of comfort.

What did the Gita say?

Most of Chapter 2 is the place to head to if your mind is restless, and unable to deal with grief and loss. With grief almost omnipresent, and so many around me grappling with loss, I went back to this chapter. Could these words from ages way past us bring us any solace and perspective? Maybe. There, in the frayed pages of my old copy of Radhakrishnan's commentary on the Gita, I tried to put together the crux of what was and has always been said, and yet, it is so difficult to understand when the moment comes.

Nevertheless, there is a soft reassurance in how gently and patiently Krishna tries to navigate us – our flustered minds and grieving hearts – through the basics of life, death, grief and loss.

In verse 11, Krishna, having heard out the distraught Arjuna, begins His response with:

> *Thou grievest for those whom thou shouldst not grieve for, and yet thou speakest words about wisdom. Wise men do not grieve for the dead or for the living.*

By those criteria, you and I have a long way to go before we can be called wise men. We think wisdom is about handling careers, situations, finances and maintaining our health. But Krishna says that wisdom means not grieving for the dead or the living.

This, to me, is on the other extreme of the emotional spectrum. In many ways, extremes seem alike, though they are driven by very different things. Like you can't see light on either end of the VIBGYOR spectrum, be it infrared (IR) or ultraviolet (UV). But IR and UV are very different. So, one way to avoid grieving for the dead or the living is to be utterly self-centered, callous and cold-hearted. The other way is to cross the emotional spectrum, reach the other side and find the wisdom to avoid grieving, not because you don't care, but because you *understand* the larger picture of the inevitability of living and dying.

In verse 13, Krishna reminds Arjuna of what He sees to be obvious:

> *As the soul passes in this body through childhood, youth and age, even so is the taking on of another body. The sage is not perplexed by this.*

We are not sages, of course, but as we proceed, He guides us further.

In verse 22, He explains:

> *Just as a person casts off worn-out garments and puts on others that are new, even so does the embodied soul cast off worn-out bodies and take on others that are new.*

After making a philosophical case from verse 11 to 25, in verse 26, He offers an alternate idea explained simply:

> *Even if thou thinkest that the self is perpetually born and perpetually dies, even then, O Arjuna, thou shouldst not grieve.*

By doing this, He attempts to come to you from opposing sides, so that no matter what position you hold in your mind, you can reconcile with this uncontrollable loss. The first line of thought is that there is no 'death'. Now, He says, even if you assume death exists, it alternates with birth.

In verse 27, Krishna softly reiterates:

> *For to one that is born, death is certain, and certain is birth for the one that has died. Therefore, for what is unavoidable, thou shouldst not grieve.*

Radhakrishnan adds a comment here – 'Our existence is brief and death is certain' – before reminding us of the tale of the grieving mother who went to the Buddha and was sent to bring a mustard seed 'from any house where no man hath yet died' and she, failing to do so, discovered that it is the law of all things that they will pass away.

I had read the aforementioned story as a child – probably in an Amar Chitra Katha comic book on the Buddha, I think. The grieving mother in the story was reminded in a humane way that she was not alone in her grief – that perhaps, in a rather sad way, grief was the one thing that bound us all. That *everyone*, every home, knows someone who has died. The only difference is that we tell ourselves that while someone lived a full life, some other person was snatched away too soon. We tell ourselves that the ones loved by God the most are taken away from us sooner. We tell ourselves all sorts of stories to calm our hearts, do we not? How many children have been told to look up at the night sky because a departed grandparent or pet is looking down at them, as a shining star? Is it not true that, in our hearts, we, even as adults, barely understand death any better than how we explain it to a four-year-old? Anything that soothes the hurt inside works for us to hold on to. Anything.

But we must try to find this wisdom before we battle this hurt, to try to be those wise men and women who 'do not grieve for the dead or the living'.

This wisdom needs to be gained with more difficulty and persistence than that required for attaining academic and professional qualifications, financial skills and street-smart reflexes. But it is perhaps more important than all of these skills and qualifications. Understanding the larger picture here is a *must* for our own emotional strength – unless we are okay with constantly living with the fear of grief, hoping that, inevitable though it is, it comes our way as late as possible. But then, we are choosing escapism and denial for something that can neither be escaped nor denied.

In verse 28, Krishna asks Arjuna, almost bereft of emotion:

> *Beings are unmanifest in their beginnings, manifest in the middles and unmanifest again in their ends, O Bharata. What is there in this for lamentation?*

In verse 30, He concludes this part of the discourse by reminding Arjuna that:

> *The dweller in the body of every one, O Bharata, is eternal and can never be slain. Therefore thou shouldst not grieve for any creature.*

These are just words when we first read them. We need to re-read, mull over, contemplate and absorb them. And that is difficult because our minds run away from this subject. We, deliberately or subconsciously, want to avoid engaging with it until it becomes a reality. At that moment, it is anyway too much to handle – we don't have the capacity to be philosophical when all we want to do is curl up and hide in a corner, nursing our grief.

Loss is intensely personal. Philosophy rarely numbs the pain, the aching of the heart. Nonetheless, there is perhaps some calmness that comes our way by going through what wiser minds, from Krishna to Vivekananda, have to share with us in their compassion. The smallest of buffers are also welcome in moments of acute pain.

2021 did not pause my association with loss, though.

June 2022 brought what I can look back on as probably the worst week of my life, emotionally speaking.

Not because of the mere fact of the loss of a parent – at my age, only a few are lucky enough to have not seen such a loss – but due to the *manner* of the loss.

My father had battled lung cancer uncomplainingly for four years, and rarely let it overwhelm him, but in a matter of a few days, the disease and its aftereffects just landed blow after unceasing blow till the frail body and still-tenacious mind could withstand no more.

Just ten days before the end, I had driven him to the airport in Delhi. He needed a little support to get out of the car, a wheelchair for the flight, and attendants to travel along with him, but other than that, he was still firmly in control of his movements, thoughts and his life. He was not very well but had still been insistent on heading back to Jammu, where he, a retired IPS officer of the J&K cadre, had spent most of his life. We agreed, even if a little unsurely.

That day was the last I saw him on his feet.

A couple of days later, I rushed to Jammu after he had been admitted to a hospital in Katra. And then, that week started. Where, every day, and then every hour, I saw his body and mind first resist, then tire out, and eventually give up. I spent hours and hours in the ICU – way more than what the rules allowed – trying to provide my father a sense of familiarity and connect amidst the first irritating and then maddening beeps of the machines that so objectively, so dispassionately, tell you the story of a body heading back to nothingness.

The most painful thing, I think, was to see the collapse of someone who had for most of his life, been in uniform, erect, even arrogant – and had then grown absolutely, utterly and pitifully dependent, not just to move around, but even for the utterly basic tasks.

For more than once – in that longest week of his life spent in the ICU – till the day he could communicate coherently, the aged, ailing individual, who was being fed via tubes, held my hand and faintly, haltingly, asked me to bring him some 'meetha'.

Multiple times a day, his throat was parched due to the flow of oxygen. He gestured over and over for a cup of water.

Clueless, frustrated and perplexed, I would look around at the nursing staff and doctors, and repeat my father's requests, asking them if there was any way of fulfilling them – only to be met, always, with quiet, disapproving nods.

How do you bring a piece of mithai to someone whose liver is failing, who is intubated and who is not even being allowed to drink water orally?

But how do you just hear such requests – so small yet so difficult to fulfill, shared with such intensity and desperation – and do nothing? 'Later, soon, when you are out of here,' you lie. At best, you moisten a piece of cloth and apply it to the patient's lips. What else can you do?

And then came a point where I could not watch my father suffer anymore, where it was clear that he would stay this way till the machines could no longer sustain his frail body. And something in me – whether driven by the Gita's soft lessons or by Vivekananda's undercurrent of not living in fear – took the decision to not let him pass in this manner.

That the 'lamentation', to use what Krishna had said, had to stop. That the soul was now passing through this body, and to fixate on keeping the body pumping via machines was not fair or kind to him anymore.

I called for an ambulance, arranged for oxygen cylinders and a few attendants at the Jammu home, and signed off on whatever I needed to state to make it clear that I was taking the decision of my own accord. Very softly, very carefully, we took my father to the ambulance. It was an hour-long drive from Katra (where the hospital was) to Jammu. Along the route, he opened his eyes for the first time in two days, and seemed to recognize me and understand that he was perhaps heading back home. When we reached Jammu and took him out of the ambulance, the paramedics holding the stretcher said to me that he had opened his eyes and had looked around, perhaps absorbing the familiar surroundings; they said he looked calm. I hoped they were right.

He was back in the room he had lived in for the past sixteen or so years, the oxygen still on, the attendants next to his bed, family members and a few old friends gathered around him. He would occasionally glance around – we did not know if he was registering anything. We stood next to the bed, softly conversing, someone or the other holding his hand.

And then, almost without realizing, in one quiet moment, a breath that he took happened to be his last. A quiet, peaceful, silent moment – deeply sad, yet not frantic, anxious or painful for him.

On his barsi, his death anniversary, we keep an assortment of mithais and water in front of his photo, and I go back to that week when a sip of water, a single piece of mithai, were his last requests. Such simple requests, from someone whom

I had seen mostly in the paraphernalia of flag cars, beacon lights, gunmen and salutes – requests that I just could not fulfill.

Will I ever forget that? Probably not.

But it is what it is.

We see life for what it is in such moments; we see all our idiotic arrogance about our jobs, cars and our influence. We see these for what they really are – completely, utterly useless when facing destiny, nature, call it what you will – and yet, as soon as we can, we forget and carry on, living just as we did, creatures of habit, prisoners of our own egos.

Death is inevitable, but helplessness is not. And it is that helplessness, that frailty, that painful-to-watch and terrible-to-endure journey to the day of final deliverance, that pinches so sharply, even years later.

May we all have the strength and understanding to absorb such pain when it afflicts those we know or, one day, if He so wills, makes its way to us.

After seeing death and grief this way, I understand more genuinely the lyrics of 'Ae Maalik Tere Bande Hum', something that I did not perhaps appreciate in my younger years:

Neki par chalein aur badi se darein,
Taaki hanste hue nikale dum.

Time dulls a few things, making us feel less intensely as days pass, but not when faced with grief or regret.

And don't we all know that?

So, what do we do? How do we come to a point where we can minimize the pain and fear?

For all own sanity and peace, and for dealing with losses that crush us, perhaps we need to go back to what Vivekananda said at the beginning of this section:

> *Often in the turmoil and struggle of our lives we seem to forget it, but suddenly some one dies — one, perhaps, whom we loved, one near and dear to our hearts is snatched away from us — and the struggle, the din and turmoil of the world around us, cease for a moment, and the soul asks the old questions 'What after this?' 'What becomes of the soul?'*

Maybe we should not forget it – the immortality of the soul – while facing turmoil and struggles?

Maybe we should find time to think about it and not wait for the moments when someone is snatched away from us. How can we make sense of a question of this magnitude amidst tears, silence, pain and a hollowness within? We can barely handle ourselves when loss and grief strike. That is not the time to comprehend philosophy. But we have time before and after, do we not?

Escaping thinking about loss and death is easy, but escaping loss itself is almost impossible. We might as well try to understand it while we are in a more 'normal' emotional headspace. Talk about it. Think about it. Read about it. Not shift the topic as soon as it comes up, not reprimand our family and friends when they talk about it. It is not a depressing topic – it is the only certainty we have in our lives. We run after what is transitional as if it is permanent, and escape and avoid thinking about what is inevitable. For how long, though?

Effort has to be put into consistently seeing the bigger picture, and to make it an integral part of the way we think and feel, so that on the day something unexpected must be handled, we don't collapse completely. Till we come to

Vivekananda's state of being, we cannot be completely stoic in the face of loss. But if we gain a sense of the larger picture, we can cope better since we are at least reassured that the person we cared for has not been *lost*. No one can be.

As Krishna tells Arjuna in verse 27:

For what is unavoidable, thou shouldst not grieve.

When I think about the fact of 'no soul being lost', for a moment, there is a half-humorous thought. What if Vivekananda himself is somewhere around, observing all this, and has a viewpoint on someone as ordinary as me trying to interpret his life's reflexes? How would I handle him ripping apart, through his impeccable and razor-sharp language, my unskilled drafting and clumsy handling of his immaculate thoughts?

Love and Bonding

What is life but growth, i.e. expansion, i.e. love? Therefore, all love is life, it is the only law of life, all selfishness is death, and this is true or hereafter... Ninety per cent of human brutes are dead, are ghosts – for none lives, my boys, but he who loves.

WHEN VIVEKANANDA SPEAKS thus of love, he is, of course, in a space that is above our everyday emotional theatre. For him, love is about not being selfish, about seeking to share the pain of others, about expanding as human beings. For most of us, love is less a universal and more a personal sentiment – one that we associate with our immediate family, our special someone, our pet, our best friends. 'Love' in that popular form is all around us – in the titles of the books we read, the plots of the movies we watch, and the tracks of the songs we hear.

Can a monk, an ascetic, teach us anything about our definition of love, which is primarily emotional attachment? Yes and no. He may not speak much about what you and I think of when we hear the words 'love', 'attachment', and so on, but he will make you reconsider the meaning of the words.

> **What is true love?**
>
> When Vivekananda speaks of love, he is in a space that is above our everyday emotional theatre. For him, love is about not being selfish, but about seeking to share the pain of others, about expanding as human beings. He says:
>
> Selfish work is slave's work; and here is a test. Every act of love brings happiness; there is no act of love which does not bring peace and blessedness as its reaction.

He explains what is *not* love, and at the very outset, you can make out that his version of love is not the one found in fairy tales, movie scripts or greeting cards.

> *The word 'love' is very difficult to understand; love never comes until there is freedom. There is no true love possible in the slave. If you buy a slave and tie him down in chains and make him work for you, he will work like a drudge, but there will be no love in him. So when we ourselves work for the things of the world as slaves, there can be no love in us, and our work is not true work. This is true of work done for relatives and friends, and is true of work done for our own selves. Selfish work is slave's work; and here is a test. Every act of love brings happiness; there is no act of love which does not bring peace and blessedness as its reaction.*

I mulled over such basics for a long time and found some sense in this when it comes to things and experiences. I 'love' going for a drive when it is raining. However, I am not sure that a cab driver who is rushing from one location to another a dozen times on a jam-packed rainy day will quite love the experience – he is doing it because it's his job, his bread for the day. The road is pretty much the same, as is the weather. We could even be driving parallel on the same road at the same point. Yet, the key differentiator would stay – I drive because I *want* to, and he drives because he *has* to. And the memories we keep of drives are of the drives we went on because we wanted to – rarely the journeys where we had to function as chauffeurs, just ferrying people around.

While drudgery and duty, whether towards people or issues, are relevant in their own way and are an inescapable part of our lives, Vivekananda suggests that we can only genuinely love those things that do not come attached with the rider that they are mandatory. If we have come to *really* love something, it does not trouble us as drudgery otherwise does. It does not make slaves out of us; we do not drag ourselves to do it, and perhaps that's where the oft-repeated thought about 'choose a job you love, and you will never have to work a day in your life', falls in sync with the monk's thoughts.

But while the love of things and experiences is one thing, the love of people is quite another. Love, in that context, is overwhelmingly seen as a synonym for romance. And the monk has his share of views here, some of which may pinch.

To begin with, see how a hundred years ago Vivekananda ripped apart obsessive, controlling behaviour masquerading as 'love'. Ask yourself if it isn't just as true today.

> *True love can never react so as to cause pain either to the lover or to the beloved. Suppose a man loves a woman; he wishes to have her all to himself and feels extremely jealous about her every movement; he wants her to sit near him, to stand near him, and to eat and move at his bidding. He is a slave to her and wishes to have her as his slave. That is not love; it is a kind of morbid affection of the slave, insinuating itself as love. It cannot be love, because it is painful; if*

she does not do what he wants, it brings him pain. With love there is no painful reaction; love only brings a reaction of bliss; if it does not, it is not love; it is mistaking something else for love.

At first cut, this sounds overly philosophical, not to say too goody-goody. What's wrong with being possessive? That's how people 'in love' behave, right? Isn't a sense of possessiveness not just accepted but even *celebrated* in popular culture as a measure of the intensity of a relationship? Have movies on infatuated, possessive love not set the cash registers ringing at the box office?

But the line between possessive and obsessive is a thin one. When you read through a month's crime news and get a sense of what people who 'love' each other can do to each other when provoked, you think about it differently. There is so much theatrical reaction, so often an absence of grace and respect, 'if she does not do what he wants'. Sometimes he is melancholy and depressed, sometimes he is violent and angry. (Of course, it is not only confined to this gender track; *she* could be angry as often when *he* does not do what she wants. Irrespective of the gender dynamics of specific relationships – in an era where society also acknowledges and celebrates the entire space of LGBTQ associations – there is a certain basic truth to the point). Love that is not reciprocated is so often the trigger for anger, stalking, and even assault. Slavish obsession, dominating control, extreme jealousy – all of that is often bundled into the larger space of what we accept as part of 'love'.

The idea of loving in such a manner that there is no reaction of pain or jealousy is neither easy nor popular or widespread. Many Indian parents tend to obsessively own their children. Families have their share of painful power struggles as kids acquire their own individuality. When children marry against parental approval, the latter may well respond emotionally, even violently. Sometimes parental love degenerates into ownership even as parents lose the capacity to differentiate between the two. Much theatre, on occasion extreme violence, follows when this sense of ownership collides with the free will of children who have now grown to be adults.

Let's accept it: we may not be able to live up to Vivekananda's ideal of what love should be, for it is a very high one.

But we can perhaps reprimand ourselves when our demonstration of love is very close to what he says it should *not* be. Is our love closer to obsession? Are we becoming control freaks? Is there more a sense of ownership than of affection? Is angst, anger, the inability to let go, to give space, the definer of most of our interpersonal equations today? Are we slaves to a relationship, and want the other to be our slave as well? Does a bond bring a sense of calm, of stability, or is it a series of emotional swings, mostly painful, that we are unable to disengage from since we are, well, 'in love'?

Then, perhaps, it is time to ask ourselves if it is, to quote Vivekananda, 'mistaking something else for love'.

On occasions, the monk in Vivekananda comes out even more sharply, with a tone that is largely unpalatable to the ideas of sentiment and emotion that we are familiar with.

I do not yet know how to respond to this, or how to absorb it in entirety. However, it merits our attention, at least, if only to know how it looked to him:

> *Surrounded by fools on every side, we think we are the only exceptions, the only learned men. Surrounded by all sorts of experiences of*

> *fickleness, we think our love is the only lasting love. How can that be? Even love is selfish, and the Yogi says that in the end we shall find that even the love of husbands and wives, and children and friends, slowly decays. Decadence seizes everything in this life. It is only when everything, even love, fails, that, with a flash, man finds out how vain, how dream-like is this world. Then he catches a glimpse of Vairâgya (renunciation).*

There is a sense of reality here, too, is there not? From movie scripts that look at heartbreak and disillusionment as the moment of realization for a central character, to tales such as that of Tulsidas who is said to have taken up the *Ramcharitmanas* after a reprimand from his wife, there is no shortage of narratives that talk of the 'flash' where people reorient their lives, when a love they had thought to be timeless eventually proved to be short-lived.

The intensity of love is rarely constant

When more intense objects of love come to us, the previous love slowly vanishes. Children think that their fathers and mothers are the dearest beings they have in their life. Then comes the husband or wife, and immediately the old feeling disappears, and the new love becomes uppermost.

– Vivekananda

Even though Vivekananda's tone and language reflect the social universe of the 1890s, being an unattached monk, he is dismissive about the routine bonds that we hold so precious. He smiles at our 'family first' basics that we hold to be unquestionable and the barbs are so sharp that they demolish the premises on which we construct popular culture:

- *Man finds out that human love is all hollow. Men cannot love though they talk about it. The wife says she loves her husband, and kisses him; but as soon as he dies, the first thing she thinks about is the bank account, and what she shall do the next day. The husband loves the wife, but when she becomes sick, and loses her beauty, or becomes haggard, or makes a mistake, he ceases to care for her. All the love of the world is hypocrisy and hollowness.*
- *We say that a wife loves her husband. She thinks that her whole soul is absorbed in him; a baby comes, and half of it goes out to the baby, or more. She herself will feel that the same love of the husband does not exist now. So with the father. We always find that when more intense objects of love come to us, the previous love slowly vanishes. Children at school think that some of their school-fellows are the dearest beings they have in life, or their fathers and mothers are so; then comes the husband or wife, and immediately the old feeling disappears, and the new love becomes uppermost.*

All human love may not be hollow, and much of this language would be close to politically incorrect stereotyping today, but he is closer to the truth than most of us would like to acknowledge. He forces us to rethink, to look back at our life, to reassess ourselves and the reflexes we take for granted.

There are other interesting situational parallels that Vivekananda draws on occasionally in talking about what is love – and, again, what is *not* love. One that held my attention was centred around Arjuna, for there are few dilemmas as acute as his. Vivekananda's approach towards 'the hell of emotionalism' is extensively shown when he starts explaining, at some length, what the problem with Arjuna was, and how even the acclaimed warrior was making a fool of himself on that account:

> *Now, Arjuna is under the control of this emotionalism. He is not what he should be – a great self-controlled, enlightened sage working through the eternal light of reason. He has become like an animal, like a baby, just letting his heart carry away his brain, making a fool of himself and trying to cover his weakness with the flowery names of 'love' and so on. Krishna sees through that. Arjuna talks like a man of little learning and brings out many reasons, but at the same time he talks the language of a fool.*

After deriding Arjuna, Vivekananda explains at length why that lapse occurred – and how we ought to shape ourselves along a line that enables us to not collapse when faced with similar, difficult choices.

Arjuna was hardly the first and will definitely not be the last individual to sound like a fool when handling moments of emotional vulnerability. But he had a very wise charioteer to slap him out of his daze and get him back on track. Most times, we don't.

We may, therefore, pay attention to what Vivekananda is trying to tell us, lest we too stumble down the path that, to us, seems like sentimental love but, to others, may appear closer to us making a fool of ourselves.

What do we take away from these unsettling, upsetting, uncomfortable lessons on love from a monk? We all will work out our own interpretations – and our ability to live according to them.

Vivekananda's concept of love: Beyond the clichés

Vivekananda's love was not the syrupy, weepy, nostalgic love of modern-day cinema and art. His love was an aggressive, combative, and a derived-from-strength emotion. It was rooted in being strong and direct; in not being merely 'sweet'. Love was not about just giving affection – it was about giving strength. His 'love' was about reaching out, and putting the interests of others ahead of our own; caring about people for what they were, not for what they could do for us, or for what emotional vacuum they could fill in our lives.

His love had no cards, no roses – no gifts attached to it.

Amidst all the clarity and the contradictions that he brought, I discovered that Vivekananda's love manifested neither in gushy romance nor in monk-like detachment. Have you seen the scene where Clint Eastwood switches off the life support of his protégé in *Million Dollar Baby*? That, to me, looked like Vivekananda's idea of love; as did the tale of the young soldier hurling himself on a live grenade so that his friends could live.

Small, intangible gestures devoid of the melodrama and grandeur of love and passion exhibited in today's world – to me, they looked like Vivekananda's idea of love.

As he says:

> *The world cares little for principles. They care for persons. They will hear with patience the words of a man they like, however nonsense, and will not listen to anyone they do not like... Your love will tell even if your words be harsh.*

This is so obvious, and yet so often we focus on the words, the language, the political correctness of things, as if they can cover the absence of caring.

And I also reverse-interpreted this to imply: your insincerity, your lack of love will tell even if your words are syrupy sweet.

Escaping 'The hell of emotionalism' and the burden of expectations

- *I wish I had nobody to love, and I were an orphan in my childhood. The greatest misery in my life has been my own people – my brothers and sisters and mother, etc...*
- *He who is alone is happy. Do good to all, like everyone, but do not love anyone. It is a bondage, and bondage brings only misery. Live alone in your mind – that is happiness. To have nobody to care for and never minding who cares for one is the way to be free.*

'I wish I had nobody to love, and I were an orphan in my childhood.'

Ouch! How do we react to that?

'To have nobody to care for and never minding who cares for one is the way to be free' – that is even more absolute. It goes against *everything* we generally hold on to. When you register a thought like that, it is massively disruptive. Your mind needs time to process it, even to register your objections to it.

Befittingly enough for a sanyasi, the *Ekla Chalo* sentiment resounds through a lot of Vivekananda's thoughts. The lines above are perhaps the strongest language he used to articulate this, but the sentiment came up recurrently over the years. As he travelled and dealt with larger numbers of people across the country and the world, and had his share of bittersweet experiences like us lesser mortals, he, too, learnt his lessons and then came to conclusions such as this:

Friendship with many is best at a distance, and everything goes well with the person who stands on his own feet.

Vivekananda has the ability to sum up extended real-life situations in single, pithy lines.

There is, of course, strength in numbers; there is the buffer of a buddy gang that turns up whenever you are in need, a gang that you can call at 4 a.m. without thinking twice. There is the sense of fulfilment of so many friends gathered together to throw you a surprise birthday party. But there is also a price to be paid after a point for 'friendship with many' – you cannot but go with the collective will, often. If you are too much of an individualist or a loner, such as I plead guilty to being, then, very soon, any 'friendship with many' begins to chafe.

I am in my forties now. For more than a decade, I have hardly spoken to anyone who was with me in primary school or when I finished school or college. The same holds true for many associates, colleagues and acquaintances of later years. One can look back at X, Y, Z as people one was comfortable having a genuine conversation with at one point of time – but, sadly enough, that's not the case anymore.

But is it actually 'sadly'? Could it have been otherwise? When associations split, or fade, one tends to have a phase of introspection and reflection. Perhaps a 21-year-old will have more energy and time to introspect on broken or atrophied associations than a 45-year-old, but both will do it. And so, when, in my twenties, I read through Vivekananda writing a letter to an associate who did not seem too fond of him anymore, I stopped at this, and then marked and then read and re-read it:

'Every meeting must have a separation' – this is the nature of things. I carry no feeling of disappointment even. I hope you will have

no bitterness. It is Karma that brings us together and Karma that separates.

It's a very interesting – even educative – thought to retain. Over the years, it grows on you.

I don't know if most of us can manage such classy separations with the people in our lives where, as we move apart, we have no disappointment and they have no bitterness. It's quite unusual – even if all celebrity interviews after their break-ups insist that they are 'still friends', most separations, whether romantic, platonic, or fraternal, aren't usually sweet.

Fairly early in life, I stopped analysing beyond a time if any association wasn't holding on. I checked the reflex to try to needlessly hold on to either individual equations or to the membership of groups. This came to a significant degree from accepting the basic thought that 'It is Karma that brings us together and Karma that separates'. I learnt to accept separations without obsessing about the whys and the hows, and to be comfortable with the inevitability of occasional emotional attrition.

The simplicity of it is that, beyond a point, we are not going to be able to 'work on' an equation – any equation. Beyond our mutual affinity, many other things contribute to our friendships – not the least the accidents of geography and time, the fact that the other person *happened* to be physically somewhere when we met. We are thrown into situations not of our making all the time. Where we live, where we study, where we work, where we travel – there is so much of chance, accident, destiny, fate, etc. – so many non-conscious choices.

So, yes, when we either connect to people or hate them – it *was* Karma that brought us together in the first place, at least in terms of the physical proximity. The same person who is indispensable to us today could have studied, lived and worked elsewhere, and never crossed our path. In that case, our life would have gone on without ever having seen each other. Random acquaintances enter our lives and then stay for decades, while on occasion we read news articles of a newlywed couple meeting with a mishap the day after the wedding, and only one surviving.

We think *we* control most of our associations, but the truth is, by choice, or by chance – in the great majority of cases, Karma will bring together, and will separate when it has to.

We have only so many years before we will be separated from everyone here – whether we loved or hated them, whether they showered us with affection or stabbed us in the back. Some bonds may well transcend that separation, but those are few and far between, and if a bond is such, instinct will tell, and there will be little need for any profound analysis and dissection in the first place.

For the rest, let Karma bring together, let it separate. Be at peace.

Let them go – accept separations

Fairly early in life, I checked the reflex to try to needlessly hold on to either individual equations or to the membership of groups. I learnt to accept separations without obsessing about the whys and hows, and to be comfortable with the inevitability of occasional emotional attrition.

In many of these (Karma-driven) separations, what is the driver? What benchmarks could we not meet?

I have often wondered at the almost mandatory elements of emotional theatre that often inhabit our lives: heartbreak, drama, accusations, tears, ecstasy, break-ups, reconciliations, unrealistic expectations, unfulfilled commitments, grand declarations, long weepy nights, sessions with possessive friends and obsessive families to resolve our emotional ups and downs.

Is the drama inevitable? Do we realize how much energy it takes out of us? Or do we just take it for granted that this is how it is?

Over the years, each time my ego was bruised or my sentiments hurt because X, Y or Z seemed ungrateful, indifferent or fickle, I was tempted to launch into pointing out how unfair that was; but then, I read and re-read the experience of Vivekananda, who permitted himself a very engaging, very human degree of angst here:

> *This is the world. What good you do goes for nothing, but if you stop doing it, then, Lord help you, you are counted as a rogue. Isn't it? Emotional natures like mine are always preyed upon by relatives and friends. This world is merciless. This world is our friend when we are its slaves and no more.*

This is not something that one should read in one go and move on. In these few sentences, a very fundamental point is being spelt out.

At 25, I did not have too much use for 'what good you do goes for nothing' since I had neither the stature nor the energy to do too much for anyone. At 35, being relatively 'senior', having had some scope to do what I mistakenly assumed would be seen as some good for some over the years, I could relate to it much more. At 40, I practically began to take it as default, and to assume that if what good you did counted for *anything* at all with the person you do it for, you should thank your stars. I concluded that the cynical saying, attributed to many, including Oscar Wilde, is largely true: No good deed goes unpunished. And learning in this way, I tried to find a balance between:

a) the reflex of stepping in when someone seemed to need it, and
b) just being an idiot with a misplaced, almost masochistic reflex of bringing sentiment into most things and, therefore, be willingly 'preyed upon by relatives and friends' and other associates

I reminded myself that if the world is merciless when it handles a Vivekananda, who did very little for himself in the years he lived, how unfair a deal am I getting? This is how it *is*.

Those of you who read about Manipur's Irom Sharmila calling off her 16-year fast would recall how the woman who was an icon among her people for years fell off the pedestal in less than a week when she spoke of wanting to finally live a 'normal' life at the age of 44. Having 'betrayed the cause', she could find no door willing to let her in. Reeling from the unanticipated hostility from people who had idolized her till a week ago, a bewildered Irom confessed in 2016, 'They want me to remain a martyr forever. But I can't always remain a martyr.'

A reminder, then, that this world is our friend when we do what it expects of us – and no more. Not even a week more. If people turn away from an icon like her the moment she doesn't play that role anymore, do the rest of us have any reason to be surprised at being disowned?

Despite all that self-lecturing, I was still sometimes hugely irked, when I put in what I thought was my most irreplaceable asset, my time, in things and situations and people, over months and years, only to find that it finally gave my words or my opinions not an ounce of greater weightage with those individuals than if I was someone they'd just met at a coffee shop a week back. People you'd genuinely invested energy in for years snapped you out of their loops in 48 hours or less if you didn't fit in with their current life plan. Over time, you realize that these are not one-off instances. And you also realize that you cannot really blame individuals who seek you out in difficult times and seek greener pastures beyond you when the difficult times have finally tided over. The trait of being 'practical' is a valued one and a hungry, street-smart practicality does not go very well with archaic sentimentalism.

Still, it can be unsettling. So what did I do? Mostly, I went back to my self-appointed Agony Uncle. And circled and highlighted and underlined this:

> *I have a mission to fulfil. I will work it out alone. I do not care who comes or who goes... Of course you are great folks now – my words will have no value with you. But I hope the time will come when you will see clearer, know better, and think other thoughts than you are doing now.*

Well, well. Reality check, everyone?

Through this, Vivekananda taught me how to respond, within my mind, to many people over time: 'You have outgrown your current needs from me, you are great folks now, and so, yes, my words will have no value with you. Let's see if a time comes when you see things clearer, in hindsight. But, frankly by then, it shouldn't even matter to me anymore.'

And so I learnt, even if slowly, to move on, rather than ruminate over the 'lack of understanding' on anyone's part. Maybe it was not them, but I, who needed to understand. If someone doesn't get it, they have the right to not get it. If, at some stage, they can, they will. If they can't, they won't. It's a capacity question. Or a personality one. There's little point getting angsty about it.

But this is about people we *want* – or wanted – to deal with. There is also the other side of it: people we *don't* want to deal with who come and tell us how to sort our lives. In my twenties, in a phase where my professional and financial state was a mess and everyone was guiding me on the 'right course', I chanced upon a fuming Vivekananda being questioned by religious gurus whether he was adhering to the appropriate diet for a sanyasi – essentially, whether he could guarantee that in foreign lands, his dietary path had not strayed from the 'pure'. I loved the tone of his response:

> *If the people in India want me to keep strictly to my Hindu diet, please tell them to send me a cook and money enough to keep him. This silly bossism without a mite of real help makes me laugh.*

'Silly bossism without a mite of real help.'

One simple sentence for the monk, one giant leap for a stress-free life.

After that, over the years, often, when distant and close relatives, random advisers, work peers, elders and seniors in various domains have raised their eyebrows or expressed their displeasure at my model of existence in general, I've:

a) thought over whether these critics would come to my aid even for a moment if I was ever in a crisis,

b) realized that in 95 per cent of the cases, the answer was no,

c) had that line replay in my head – *silly bossism without a mite of real help* – and thereafter proceeded to pay no attention to their opinion, leaving it to muscle fatigue and gravity to bring their raised eyebrows down in due course.

> I am determined to get rid of all sentimentalism and emotionalism, and hang me if you ever find me emotional.
>
> – Vivekananda

I also owe Vivekananda so much simply for the fact that it's very difficult to guilt-trip or emotionally blackmail me into doing anything. It's equally difficult to push or jostle me into agreeing to things. It's also a tough task to scare me with the ramifications of anything I do on anyone else. When I do find myself slipping sometimes down a hyper-emotional slope, I quickly turn the pages of my worn-out *Letters Of Swami Vivekananda* till I find the lines I have marked very vividly, to remind myself of this sentiment:

> *I am determined to get rid of all sentimentalism and emotionalism, and hang me if you ever find me emotional.*

We can't decide when people live or die. Don't selectively thrust that role onto our conscience, or make us that important. Whether it is a relative, friend, or colleague, we can't *give* anyone a heart attack or low BP. Not unless *they* want to react in an extreme manner. Equally, let us not give anybody the power to give us a heart attack.

As Erica Jong puts it:

Take your life in your own hands and what happens? A terrible thing: No one to blame!

Is that being insensitive? Maybe. Or is it just acquired common sense?

This was a sentiment – if that word can be used for the idea of not being sentimental – that Vivekananda came back to again, in even sharper terms, as time went by.

> *Don't for a moment worry on my account. 'Mother' looks after me. She is bringing me fast out of the hell of emotionalism, and bringing me into the light of pure reason.*

One may not reach the zone of pure reason in an average lifetime, but at least one can begin to understand that being a weepy, messy, can't-ever-say-no, over-sweet person, isn't being 'nice'. It's just habit. Being overly sentimental 24/7 isn't going to have the world thanking you, because it's unsustainable, and the moment you finally tire of it, you're going to be branded as the villain. You might as well be the villain at the outset itself.

At least your life is simpler.

Lessons on attachment vs. detachment

That man alone will be able to get the best of nature, who, having the power of attaching himself to a thing with all his energy, has also the power to detach himself when he should do so. The difficulty is that there must be as much power of attachment as that of detachment.

– Vivekananda

This does not mean he asks us to be indifferent to emotion and pain. There is a difference between not being vulnerable to 'emotional nonsense' and being apathetic.

> *That man alone will be able to get the best of nature, who, having the power of attaching himself to a thing with all his energy, has also the power to detach himself when he should do so. The difficulty is that there must be as much power of attachment as that of detachment. There are men who are never attracted by anything. They can never love, they are hard-hearted and apathetic; they escape most of the miseries of life. But the wall never feels the misery, the wall never loves, is never hurt; but it is the wall, after all…*

Vivekananda sets tough benchmarks – that one must have the power to be attached *as well as* to be detached. We may not meet them perfectly in our lifetime – but the more we try, and the closer we get to it, the calmer our life will probably be.

Before wrapping up this topic, I will make a small reference to a lesson on this that I learnt from Ramakrishna, when I read up on him as an extension of my curiosity about Vivekananda's thinking. I quote it because this advice from the epitome of renounced monastic living has been a very practical, pragmatic part of my middle-class householder's life, when it comes to both handling as well as having expectations.

Ramakrishna had advised his disciples on the basics of detachment along these lines:

- *As a wet-nurse in a wealthy family brings up her master's child, loving it as if it were her own, yet knowing well that she has no claim upon it, so you also think that you are but trustees and guardians of your children whose real father is the Lord Himself.*
- *The maid-servant says with reference to her master's house, 'This is our house.' All the while she knows that the house is not her own, and that her own house is far away in a distant village of Burdwan or Nadia. Her thoughts are all really directed to her village home. Again, referring to her master's child in her arms, she says, 'My Hari has grown very naughty,' or 'My Hari likes to eat this or that,' and so on. But all the while she knows for certain that Hari is not her own. I tell those who come to me, to lead a life unattached like the maid-servant. I tell them to live unattached to this world – to be in the world, but not of the world – and at the same time to have their mind directed to God, the heavenly home whence all come.*

This is a great reference point each time one is caught up in the complexities of life that come from an exaggerated sense of 'my' work, 'my' job, 'my' child, my whatever.

In particular, I have taken Ramakrishna's words very literally so far as being just a trustee of my children is concerned. What school they got into, what marks they got, how well they did or did not do at assorted activities, what subjects, what college – almost all of these I left to their academic abilities and the guidance of their teachers. I have *observed* rather than participated in that process. Will my children take career option X or Y? I *advise*, as an impartial observer, if they want my opinion, but I neither expect nor demand.

I have very few expectations, very little desire to live my life's unfulfilled dreams through the next generation, and am very comfortable with a general sense of being a detached witness to their lives, even while being present whenever required. The mental picture of a nurse holding someone else's child – *caring* enough to keep it well but not *owning* it – has always stayed in my mind. A detached, hopefully responsible but certainly non-possessive reflex of parenting has been a great value addition to my thirties and forties.

And you can extend it to other associations as well – we can play God neither to the generation that comes after us, nor the one before us.

Vivekananda, too, remembered this message of his master and conveyed it ahead.

> *My Master used to say, 'Look upon your children as a nurse does'. The nurse will take your baby and fondle it and play with it and behave towards it gently as if it were her own child; but as soon as you give her notice to quit she is ready to start off bag and baggage… Everything in the shape of attachment is forgotten; it will not cause the ordinary nurse the least pang to leave your children and take up other children. Even so are you to be with all that you consider your own. You are the nurse, and if you believe in God, believe that all these things which you consider yours are really His.*

In 2019, one of my children was giving the Class X boards, while the other was giving Class XII exams. I have always been told that these exams are more a test of the parents than of the students. But I have, for over 15 years now, trained my mind to remember that I am the caretaker, not the owner of their lives and destinies. I do not sell myself the fiction that I can 'shape their lives'. And so, I waltzed through their dual 'Board year' barely registering that it was any different from routine, apart from some sleep lost on account of early morning chauffeur duties on the actual exam dates.

Through the year, I did not want to trip from my default reflex. I did what I had to, but with very little micro monitoring, very little obsessing about how things will go, without letting my blood pressure shoot up on any academic issue. And so, as that year came to a close, and on the day they finished their exams, I felt I too had passed my test. In all objectivity, I had played the nurse fairly well, as well as I had for the decade gone by. Both my children have entered career tracks of their own choice. I have mostly just watched what they opted to do, neither discouraging nor patronizing. They are doing all right. I think it is an important lesson in parenting – of neither taking on nor having too many expectations.

And for that, again, I have only Vivekananda to thank, for he taught me how to deal with others. I'll attempt to sum up the essence of his 'people philosophy':

- He had a very unusual approach towards explaining affection and love. It makes you question your basics. He dismisses overly possessive equations of love, where 'He is a slave to her and wishes to have her as his slave'. That 'cannot be love', he says. If *that* is the sort of bond you are in, and if jealousy, obsession, and control are key elements of your love, he asks you to question whether you are 'mistaking something else for love'.

- Are you overly miserable for what could have been? Or do you carry an excessive emotional burden of equations that did not fully form, or broke off? He brings you another perspective: 'It is Karma that brings together and Karma that separates', and asks you to remember that 'Every meeting must have a separation – that is the nature of things'.
- Do you occasionally have the sense that being excessively sentimental or sensitive works to your disadvantage? He often reminded himself to keep away from 'the hell of emotionalism', a key reminder for us as well. My learning is that to be chronically vulnerable to emotional blackmail is an exhausting way to live – and one can opt out.
- There is plenty of unsolicited advice in your twenties and thirties, especially in India. It comes close to becoming an instruction, while some of it is pitched as your 'duty'. We usually sulk, but do it anyway. But he taught me not to give much weightage to 'silly bossism without a mite of real help'. It was very liberating.
- Do you expect gratitude forever? Do you think you had invested energy, effort, and are then shown the door once your utility is over, or judged when you simply didn't have energy left to invest, anymore? When I thought that way, Vivekananda's sentiments reminded me that, 'This is the world. What good you do goes for nothing.' If you pause, you're promptly declared a villain. Well, if this is how it is, why mull over it beyond a point?
- He teaches a key lesson his Master taught him – don't be over-possessive about the next generation and don't live your dreams through them. 'Look upon your children as a nurse does' – take good care of them, but do not *own* them. Be prepared to let go, if needed, without excessive trauma.

Key Takeaways

'Misery dares not approach us – till the mind is weakened'

> *The weak have no place here, in this life or in any other life. Weakness leads to slavery. Weakness leads to all kinds of misery, physical and mental. Weakness is death. There are hundreds of thousands of microbes surrounding us, but they cannot harm us unless we become weak, until the body is ready and predisposed to receive them. There may be a million microbes of misery, floating about us. Never mind! They dare not approach us, they have no power to get a hold on us, until the mind is weakened. This is the great fact: strength is life, weakness is death. Strength is felicity, life eternal, immortal; weakness is constant strain and misery: weakness is death.*

Over and over, through all that he says, Vivekananda comes back to this core point. And it becomes the test when there is a question that we are unable to resolve: which of the options before me will make me weaker from within? That weakening will bring only 'constant strain and misery'; it's better to suffer short-term problems – physical, social, financial – than to weaken the mind.

Build mental and emotional immunity

Work on yourself and your mind to develop the level of strength so that no matter what floats around, it doesn't impact your mind, just the way most microbes can do little if your physical fitness and immunity levels are strong.

When you have no time or energy to engage in a detailed analysis, when the intellect is too caught up in loops of logic, disengage, and ask yourself: which decision will leave you feeling weaker within? Identify it – and then walk away from it. And don't look back.

Whatever you face that stresses you, remember the point Vivekananda makes about microbes and your immunity (the coronavirus doesn't seem to be respectful of *any* degree of immunity, but even then, the exception does not negate the rule, does it?). You may not like the volume of traffic around you when you drive, but that is not going to change. You may not like the amount of politics at your workplace, and that is not going to change, either. You may not like the vibes you have with your immediate relatives, but if it hasn't been sorted in all these years, it is unlikely to transform now.

What is floating around you is *not* in your hands, but the way you surmount your vulnerability and your lack of immunity definitely is. Work on yourself and on your mind to develop the level of strength so that no matter *what* floats around, it doesn't impact your mind. Just the way most microbes can do little if your physical fitness and immunity is strong. Even if we cannot be absolutely invincible – some situations and some viruses *will* be potent enough to get past – building a high degree of resistance will at least enable us to lead most of our life in a stable manner, without it resembling a recurrent collapse-and-recovery model.

'Be in no hurry to give your thoughts to others... first *have* something to give'

In my early years, as I read a lot about Vivekananda, while attempting to grasp the Gita, and consuming Yogananda as well as other streams of thought, I wondered why people didn't share my interests. Charged with all this newly-acquired knowledge, I engaged in discussions and debates, wrote letters, sent books to friends, and conversed endlessly if I thought someone had completely missed the point of existence.

As I entered the workspace, I often extended that reflex to lecture those hapless souls working with me. My Vivekananda-inspired obsession with *how* we work being more important than *what* we do at work translated into endless amounts of unsolicited advice to people on why the way they were approaching work was not the way to grow. I questioned, reprimanded, cajoled, and wondered why someone would put anything less than their life's blood into what they took up, no matter what it was, for was it not more a question of their *own* growth and the evolution of their personalities, than about turning up to earn a day's salary and meet office targets?

Like all unsolicited advice, whether to a teenaged child or to a young employee, it was often not welcome. I also suspect, in hindsight, that it did not fit in with any rational understanding of a work–life balance in their minds.

Work on yourself, be in no hurry to teach

It is not our duty to dispense unsolicited wisdom, assuming that it is wisdom in the first place! Our task is to work on ourselves, to keep on working, and be content to leave it there, not to act as uninvited vocal crusaders for our beliefs and causes.

After inflicting much of my unsolicited wisdom on unwilling listeners over the years, at a recent point in time (probably far later than I ought to have), I paid greater attention to Vivekananda on the following:

> *This man (Ramakrishna) sought no one. His principle was, first form character, first earn spirituality and results will come of themselves. His favourite illustration was, 'When the lotus opens, the bees come of their own accord to seek the honey; so let the lotus of your character be full-blown, and the results will follow.' This is a great lesson to learn.*
>
> *My master taught me this lesson hundreds of times, yet I often forget it. Few understand the power of thought. If a man goes into a cave, shuts himself in, and thinks one really great thought and dies, that thought will penetrate the walls of that cave, vibrate through space, and at last penetrate the whole human race. Such is the power of thought; be in no hurry therefore to give your thoughts to others. First have something to give…therefore first make character – that is the highest duty you can perform. Know Truth for yourself, and there will be many to whom you can teach it afterwards; they will all come. This was the attitude of my master.*

The only thing I can claim to have in common with Vivekananda is that, just like him, *my* master taught me this lesson hundreds of times, yet I, too, often forget it.

To 'be in no hurry to give your thoughts to others' is a difficult lesson to learn, as we are prone to overestimating both our comprehension of ideas and others' interest in those ideas. We read but do not register fully, for we are all too full of ourselves, and no sooner than we have done or learnt anything beyond the rudimentary, we cannot help ourselves from picking up the megaphone and telling the world around us all about it.

In my forties, however fleetingly, I have attempted to cut this reflex even further, and tried not to fall into this recurrent error of being in a hurry to give my thoughts, for whatever they are worth. It is not our duty to dispense unsolicited wisdom, assuming that it is wisdom in the first place! Our task is to work on ourselves, to keep on working, and be content to leave it there, not to act as uninvited vocal crusaders for our beliefs and causes. We must check ourselves each time we seem to be in an unseemly hurry to give our thoughts to others, to lecture, to philosophize, to inflict on others our worldview no matter how disinterested the hapless recipients may be, merely because we happen to be 'seniors' in age, relationship, work or any other capacity. If our thoughts are distilled enough, and if they are indeed of any use to anyone, as Ramakrishna told his disciple, 'they will all come'.

Vivekananda himself travelled across the seas in the 1890s, with little money and little knowledge of the places where he was headed, but in each country where he landed as an unknown, distrusted entity, they all came. They came not because he distributed pamphlets and had a great marketing team, but because he had something to give, because he had worked on *himself* intensely, unforgivingly, for years.

Incidentally, at a later point in time, Vivekananda summed up Ramakrishna's life this way, which is almost the same thought rephrased:

> *The first part of my Master's life was spent in acquiring spirituality, and the remaining years in distributing it.*

Before we seek to distribute, let us first acquire.

Every parent, every boss, every self-anointed philosopher, advisor and well-wisher needs to occasionally be reminded of this thought, since all of us are prone to forget it. Whatever your zone of interest is – metaphysics or music – *be in no hurry to teach.* First *have* something to give.

I do realize that those who have endured endless hours of painful lectures at my hands will laugh out loud at this part, but I hope they will also acknowledge that I now am in less and less of a hurry to teach anyone anything as each year passes. Perhaps you, too, have done something similar – have been in a hurry to give your thoughts to others, more so now that we have so many ways to tell the whole world what we feel and think, about anything and everything. Our phone is now our megaphone.

Perhaps it is time to see if you are in a 'hurry to teach'.

His religion was not political, neither were his teachings

> *I have considered the matter most carefully and have come to the conclusion that of those who profess and talk of religion nowadays in this country, the majority are full of morbidity – crack-brained or fanatic.*

This is as good a place as any for me remind us all that Vivekananda was not a religious fanatic and held an extremely unflattering viewpoint on this kind of fanaticism. His words are direct and blunt:

> *Is there one universal philosophy? Not yet. Each religion brings out its own doctrines and insists upon them as being the only true ones. And not only does it do that, but it thinks that he who does not believe in them must go to some horrible place. Some will even draw the sword to compel others to believe as they do. This is not through wickedness, but through a particular disease of the human brain called fanaticism. They are very sincere, these fanatics, the most sincere of human beings; but they are quite as irresponsible as other lunatics in the world. This disease of fanaticism is one of the most dangerous of all diseases. All the wickedness of human nature is roused by it. Anger is stirred up, nerves are strung high, and human beings become like tigers.*

Similarly, Vivekananda had little respect for 'religious anger':

> *Our religion teaches that anger is a great sin, even if it is 'righteous'. Each must follow his own religion. I could not for my soul distinguish ever the distinction between 'religious anger' and 'commonplace anger', 'religious killing' and 'commonplace killing', 'religious slandering and irreligious', and so forth. Nor may that 'fine' ethical distinction ever enter into the ethics of our nation!*

There are times when Vivekananda is portrayed as some deeply-dyed-in-saffron monk, or as someone who had no mission other than portraying the greatness of the country he was born in. That does not do him justice. For Vivekananda's mind was evolved enough and elastic enough to understand that the strengths of the philosophy that this land had bred and the manner in which the people of the land managed to live by them were hardly synonymous; indeed, at times, they were polar opposites. Though he deeply loved his motherland, he had not the least notion of any inherent *superiority* for his fellow countrymen, and he was not in the least engaged in the political questions of the day.

> I do not believe in any politics. God and truth are the only politics in the world, everything else is trash.
>
> – Vivekananda

As he lived and learnt and travelled and reflected, the monk who is often – to my mind, erroneously – pitched primarily as an icon of 'Indian-ness' did *not* make the mistake of assuming that the mental universe of the land of his birth was superior to all else. It is a little mystifying to see his name occasionally being treated primarily as a synonym of national pride, culture, history, etc. – as if a political line, as if *any* political line, is in sync with how he thought.

> *I do not believe in any politics. God and truth are the only politics in the world, everything else is trash.*

Since I have briefly mentioned Vivekananda's travels and reflections, allow me an indulgence. I want to make you quickly read through the one thing that everyone associates with him in the context of his global travels.

The Chicago address

It has been over 130 years since Vivekananda gave his brief yet iconic speech. Almost everyone who has heard of Vivekananda has also heard the words 'the Chicago address'. We take pride in the fact that he spoke there and that his words had such an impact. But have we read through those words ourselves? Have we actually understood what he told the world about the religion he practiced?

Let us take a couple of minutes then to refresh our memories of what he *actually* said, since sometimes this address tends to be forgotten after 'Brothers and sisters of America' – just the way the crux of his life's teachings often tends to be condensed on social media to 'Arise, awake and stop not till the goal is reached'.

Allow me also the indulgence of highlighting some portions of Vivekananda's address, for it appealed to the audience because it was such a clear continuation of Ramakrishna's philosophy. It was an emphatic declaration of tolerance, universal brotherhood and a desire that the 'death-knell of all fanaticism' be the convention:

> *Sisters and Brothers of America,*
> *It fills my heart with joy unspeakable to rise in response to the warm and cordial welcome which you have given us. I thank you in the name of the most ancient order of monks in the world, I thank you in the name of the mother of religions, and I thank you in the name of millions and millions of Hindu people of all classes and sects.*
>
> *My thanks, also, to some of the speakers on this platform who, referring to the delegates from the Orient, have told you that these men from far-off nations may well claim the honor of bearing to different lands the idea of toleration. I am proud to belong to a religion which has taught the world both tolerance and universal acceptance. We believe not only in universal toleration, but we accept all religions as true. I am proud to belong to a nation which has sheltered the persecuted and the refugees of all religions and all nations of the earth. I am proud to tell you that we have gathered in our bosom the purest remnant of the Israelites, who came to Southern India and took refuge with us in the very year in which their holy temple was shattered to pieces by Roman tyranny. I am proud to belong to the religion which has sheltered and is still fostering the remnant of the grand Zoroastrian nation. I will quote to you, brethren, a few lines from a hymn which I remember to have repeated from my earliest boyhood, which is every day repeated by millions of human beings:*

> *'As the different streams having their sources in different paths which men take through different tendencies, various though they appear, crooked or straight, all lead to Thee.'*
>
> *The present convention, which is one of the most august assemblies ever held, is in itself a vindication, a declaration to the world of the wonderful doctrine preached in the Gita: 'Whosoever comes to Me, through whatsoever form, I reach him; all men are struggling through paths which in the end lead to me.' Sectarianism, bigotry, and its horrible descendant, fanaticism, have long possessed this beautiful earth. They have filled the earth with violence, drenched it often and often with human blood, destroyed civilization and sent whole nations to despair. Had it not been for these horrible demons, human society would be far more advanced than it is now. But their time is come; and I fervently hope that the bell that tolled this morning in honor of this convention may be the death-knell of all fanaticism, of all persecutions with the sword or with the pen, and of all uncharitable feelings between persons wending their way to the same goal.*

I have not read a louder, more straightforward taking down of religion fanaticism – from a monk dressed in a grand robe, speaking on a foreign platform, summarizing what his land's religious philosophy was.

'Sectarianism, bigotry, and its horrible descendant, fanaticism … have filled the earth with violence, drenched it often and often with human blood, destroyed civilization and sent whole nations to despair.'

That is what he said. That is what he believed.

In an earlier chapter, I had made the point that when people saw that I was a 'follower' of Vivekananda and I was accused, therefore, of being 'religious', I was quick to deny that charge. It is also important to deny the insinuation that 'following' Vivekananda implies being a proponent of any one culture or ideology.

Many proclaim loudly that they are very proud of him; that he was a great son of India. We can be very proud of all he stood for, that is one thing. Whether *he* was very proud of all that *we* stood for, at least while he lived, whether we can be proud of ourselves for living along the lines he would have demanded of us – *that* is something we should not take for granted. If we are proud of him delivering that address, we should occasionally ask ourselves if we are living and practicing our religion along the lines he spoke of when he was representing us that day in Chicago.

Tough love

Vivekananda was a practitioner of what is popularly referred to as 'tough love' today. He was unforgiving of shortcomings, whether of his disciples or the people of the country. He loved his land and his faith dearly, but he was harsh in pointing out flaws wherever he saw them. His love was not blind or fanatical.

Vivekananda was a practitioner of what is popularly referred to as 'tough love' today. He was unforgiving of shortcomings, whether of his disciples or the people of the country he wished to see great, but could clearly see – and say – that there was a long way to go yet. He loved his land and his faith dearly, but he was harsh in pointing out flaws wherever he saw them. His love was not blind or fanatical.

He was *not* asking us to assume that we are the greatest civilization in the world even if we are the oldest. He was *not* asking us to believe that the brilliance of the theory of our spiritual lineage makes up for deficiencies in practice. He was *not* asking us to mistake temples and rituals with what religion means, even if he was a formally ordained monk. He was *not* asking us to obsess primarily with political freedom and to assume that the English vacating the land and letting us govern it would make us superior to them or miraculously free us of our flaws.

Speaking about Ramakrishna, he said:

> *The Vedas can only be explained and the Shastras reconciled by his theory of Avastha or stages – that we must not only tolerate others, but positively embrace them, and that truth is the basis of all religions.*

Vivekananda was, above all, a spiritual mind with a global vision. His ideology belongs to all, irrespective of nationality or faith. If you see him in any other light, it is perhaps time to read about him – and of Ramakrishna – afresh.

'The older I grow, the more everything seems to me to lie in manliness'

There is one index I have used in the past few years, mostly in my forties, to get a sense of whether or not I have understood anything of Vivekananda's teachings.

And that is whether my frequency of referring to him is reducing.

I first realized this was happening in the course of the assorted pieces I wrote about him over the past 15-odd years, and while referring to the notes for this book that I have been compiling off and on for some years now. The tone kept changing over time. As a writer, that caused me – and a potential publisher – some distress, because to come back to things or topics is easier if you are thinking just the way you did when you wrote the first draft. But as an individual, that change, that disconnect to some things I connected to earlier, that diminishing of the need to refer to guidance, that creeping in of a tone that was 'more about how you think than about how Vivekananda did' – that gradual shift was very educative. It was, when I understood it, just a bit of growing up, or outgrowing.

And as I saw it happening, I acknowledged, and appreciated the brilliance of Vivekananda as a teacher.

Throughout his life he explained that the point of lives of the incarnations themselves, lives such as Christ and Buddha, was not about worshipping their *personalities* but about absorbing their lives, about seeing them as people who lived a path and showed us how to live that as well, if we choose to, wholly or partially.

He worshipped Ramakrishna unquestioningly *after* he doubted him intensely:

> *Let none regret that they were difficult to convince! I fought my Master for six years with the result that I know every inch of the way! Every inch of the way!*

He shied away from asking the world to accept Ramakrishna's personality or from creating a sect centred on him, and asked nothing more than that his message be spread far and wide. He questioned everything, everyone, and recurrently and sharply slammed the instinct of unthinking obedience to a cause, belief or person, no matter how great. He trashed mindless adherence to rituals or practices merely because they had been practised for centuries. He was not 'God-fearing'; indeed, he did not think that you could get anywhere close to God if you were the 'fearing' sort of person in the first place.

He was also anything but a believer in the wisdom of numbers: 'What you call majority is mainly composed of fools and men of common intellect. Men who have brains to think for themselves are few, everywhere' is hardly a lesson in political correctness. Over and over, he reiterated his disdain for judging a person, or an idea, on the basis of what the 'majority' view was on a given day. On some days, he was gentle and compared the masses to children who have yet to understand things, on others, he was sharper and less forgiving of 'common intellect'.

Vivekananda did not look to make 'followers'. He did not take pride in either his Master or him being venerated as individuals. Through what he said and through what he lived, he reiterated, over and over again:

- Do *not* worship an idea, a guru, a teacher, a master, however great, *unquestioningly*
- Do *not* accept an idea, a thought, a practice, no matter how popular, how ancient, how widespread, *unquestioningly*

Stand not with folded hands and bowed heads before either the grandeur of a personality, or the weight of popular opinion, is what Vivekananda says to me through the story of his life. Think for yourself.

An icon for all

- Vivekananda was, above all, a spiritual mind with a global vision. His ideology belongs to all, irrespective of nationality or faith.
- Vivekananda did not look to make 'followers'. He did not take pride in either his Master or him being venerated as individuals. He reiterated: Do not worship an idea or guru however great, unquestioningly. Do not accept an idea, a thought, a practice, no matter how ancient, how widespread, unquestioningly.

And so, as time went by, I realized that the more I 'followed' him and subconsciously absorbed bits and pieces of his basics, the more the idea of 'following' began to seem, well, not really something to aspire to. By absorbing what Vivekananda was hammering into my mind day after day, without it even being a conscious effort, I learned to not blindly believe in unquestioned, indisputable truths but instead to evaluate doubt. I learned to stay cynical, and to consistently question and ask; to not be God-fearing, but to find the idea of being afraid of God a very pedestrian one.

From this Man of God I learned to not blindly trust the word or wisdom of any Man of God just because he had masses of followers.

From the saffron-clad monk I learned to not leave to saffron-clad men the interpretation of my life's rights and wrongs just because they wore saffron. Or, for that matter, white. Or black.

Almost imperceptibly, I realized that the *less* blindly I hero-worshipped him, the greater was his victory in transforming my thought. After all, does the victory of a philosophy lie in the need of the follower to keep following, instead of mastering the thought itself? No!

Find your own answers

From this Man of God I learned to not blindly trust the word or wisdom of any Man of God just because he had masses of followers. From the saffron-clad monk, I learnt to not leave to saffron-clad men the interpretation of my life's rights and wrongs just because they wore saffron. Or white. Or black.

Small minds, fragile egos and little leaders need that every word of theirs be unquestionably worshipped.

But the evolved mind of a true leader – and leadership of thought is the greatest – looks to go beyond the master–servant bond; it looks to engage with you as an equal, to have you think for yourself, and leaves the final call to you.

As Krishna did with Arjuna.

And so being a 'follower' of the monk, hands folded in reverence, is not the primary instinct anymore. Because age is now catching up, perhaps, I am now increasingly captivated by the drama and the flamboyance of this Vivekananda thought, a thought I have referred to earlier as well:

> *The older I grow, the more everything seems to me to lie in manliness. This is my new gospel. Do even evil like a man. Be wicked, if you must, on a grand scale!*

The older I grow, the more everything about following Vivekananda seems to lie in understanding the probing, challenging and questioning message of his life – not in being a disciple, not in waving incense sticks around his picture, not in being a clerical follower of his writings and a faithful, unquestioning recipient of all his teachings.

I have begun to think that perhaps the only way to truly 'follow' Vivekananda is to, over time, outgrow the instinct of 'following' itself.

About the Author

Anshul Chaturvedi is a veteran editor with almost 30 years of experience in print media, which he has spent observing everything, from politics to cinema.

He came across Swami Vivekananda's works when he was 16. Later, in hindsight, he realized what Subhas Bose had meant when he wrote: 'I was barely fifteen when Vivekananda entered my life. Then there followed a revolution within, and everything was turned upside down.'

He has written about Vivekananda's teachings for various platforms, including *Speaking Tree* and his blog, for over 15 years.

When not earning his daily bread, he spends his time reading about WW2 and managerial philosophy, and binge-watching police procedurals. Currently based in Noida, he works as an executive editor with *The Times of India*. You can follow him on X @AnshulChaturvdi.